Corporate Diversification:
Entry, Strategy, and Performance

Corporate
Diversification:

 This book won the Richard D. Irwin Prize
for the Best Doctoral Dissertation 1975-76
at the Harvard Business School

Published by the Division of Research
   Graduate School of Business Administration
   Harvard University
   Boston, MA   02163

Entry, Strategy, and Performance

E. Ralph Biggadike

Associate Professor
Darden Graduate School
of Business Administration
University of Virginia

Order from Harvard University Press
79 Garden Street
Cambridge, MA 02138 • London, England

Library of Congress Cataloging in Publication Data

Biggadike, E. Ralph, 1937–
  Corporate diversification.
  Bibliography: p.
  Includes index.
  1. Diversification in industry—United States.
2. New products—United States. 3. Conglomerate corp-
orations—United States. I. Harvard University.
Graduate School of Business Administration. Division
of Research. II. Title.
HD2756.U5B53   338.8   79-84159
ISBN 0-87584-118-X

*Text type set in Caledonia by DEKR Corporation. Printed in the United
States of America by Halliday Lithograph.*

Foreword

Stimulated in part by the increasing predominance of large multiproduct, multinational firms in the world's economy, the subject of strategic planning has emerged as a major management concern. Growth through diversification into product-markets where the firm has not previously competed ranks with planning for existing activities as a top planning priority.

Yet in spite of its relative importance, new entry has not received anything like its fair share of attention as a subject for scientific inquiry. Advances in strategic planning in the last decade have concentrated on strategies for existing businesses—particularly on ways to discriminate between businesses with respect to growth, market share, net income, ROI, and cash flow objectives.[1]

Entry into product-markets unfamiliar to the parent company has also received relatively little attention compared to the new product development process at one extreme and broad problems of corporate diversification at the other. In between these two extremes, at the level of the individual business unit, there are gaping holes in our knowledge.

How successful are start-up businesses in terms of financial performance and market share? How long do they typically take to achieve positive returns and to perform comparably with existing businesses? What entry strate-

---

1. See, for example, George S. Day, "Diagnosing the Product Portfolio," *Journal of Marketing* (April 1977), pp. 29–38.

gies are used by new start-up businesses, and what factors explain their particular performance?

The research reported in this book answers these questions and sheds needed light on the problem of new entry. This particular study was conducted as part of a broader research effort in the area of strategic planning conducted at the Harvard Business School, the Marketing Science Institute, and the Strategic Planning Institute[2] over the last several years—an effort which continues today. Other activities include clinical studies dealing with various aspects of existing business strategy—in particular how to define the business as a starting point of strategic planning.

These research efforts all have a common thread—a thread which is exemplified in this study by Ralph Biggadike. They are built on conceptual frameworks drawn from three different but closely related disciplines: marketing, business policy, and industrial organization economics. Cross-fertilization between these three disciplines is opening up new and interesting ways of thinking about business strategy and market structures. As a result, the development of each individual discipline, as well as the development of strategic planning, is undergoing a fundamental shift. Both managers and those concerned with public policy towards industry have a vital interest in the emerging new concepts and empirical results.

This particular study draws on the experience of forty business units that entered product-markets new to their parent company, as well as on a somewhat larger sample of businesses already submitting data to the PIMS project. These two samples are used to compute a variety of measures of financial and market performance two, four, and eight years after entry. The results are likely to cause more than raised eyebrows in corporate offices and boardrooms—on average, for example, entrant businesses need eight years to become profitable. Performance differs considerably depending on the relatedness between the new entrant and its parent, the market entered, the entry strat-

---

2. See Sidney Schoeffler, Robert D. Buzzell, and Donald F. Heany, "Impact of Strategic Planning on Profit Performance," *Harvard Business Review* (March–April 1974), pp. 137–145.

egy, and the reaction of competitors already in the business. Biggadike's conclusion is that the over-all poor results of these samples stem largely from a failure to set sufficiently aggressive goals or to enter on a sufficiently large scale.

Apart from providing management with a much needed set of benchmarks for new entry performance, Biggadike's work marks an important step forward in conceptualizing the problem of new entry. Strategic alternatives in terms of directions for corporate diversification, scale of entry, trade offs between long run market performance and short run financial performance, and marketing strategy, are suggested for various types of market situations which the firm may enter. Of central importance is the conclusion that management must be *explicit* about its goals ahead of time. In this sense, Biggadike's conclusions complement contemporary thinking about strategies for existing businesses, particularly the recognition that different strategic roles in terms of growth, share, income, ROI, and cash flow may be assigned to different businesses depending on market opportunity and company resources.

Much remains to be learned about strategic planning and planning for new entry in particular. This book lays important groundwork for this task by establishing a conceptual scheme and by providing practitioners with quantified measures of actual performance.

DEREK F. ABELL
Harvard Business School
Vevey, Switzerland
May 1979

Preface

This book is about corporate diversification at the business unit level. The research does not study the total corporation; instead it looks at the subunit of the corporation that made the diversification attempt. Furthermore, the research does not study entry into broadly defined industries (for example, Census Bureau two-, three-, or even four-digit industries—many of which are irrelevant to business administration decisions). It does address the segment of the industry—often referred to as the "served market"— that the business unit entered. The research studies both internally developed businesses and acquired businesses and follows their vicissitudes for the first eight years of their commercialization. I believe these research findings are the first about the early years of diversification at this lower organizational and narrower market level.

To most executives cooperating in the study, the findings were initially surprising. The findings were and still remain disconcerting. It is therefore particularly appropriate in this preface both to emphasize limitations to the study and also to report subsequent events which should raise the readers' confidence in what they are about to read.

The sample size is small (forty businesses) relative to the number of explanatory variables in my model. Originally, seventy businesses were in the sample, but the research coincided with the 1974–1975 recession. Many executives found it impractical to help me gather the data and withdrew from the project. Furthermore, much of the data are skewed and do not, therefore, satisfy the normality assumption of multivariate analysis. These characteristics prevented a multivariate examination of all the variables influencing performance. Consequently, most of the analysis examines the influence of one factor at a time. For example, I demonstrate that entrant businesses with higher relative prices had poorer financial performance than those that matched competitors' prices. Lacking a multivariate analysis, I can only suggest that future entrants should set their entry prices closer to competitors'. This limitation should be borne in mind when reading chapters 6–10. In chapter 11, I attempt to lessen this limitation by linking the individual findings.

On the other hand, the findings have withstood two subsequent tests. First, they have met a "face validity" test from a few hundred executives who have viewed, studied, and discussed them. I estimate, for example, that on average it takes corporate ventures eight years to become profitable. Executives' initial reaction to this finding is one of disbelief. Later, after having reviewed their other diversification experiences, most executives conclude the eight-year estimate is uncomfortably probable. I cannot cite these anecdotes but can point to several cases in the public domain where this is so. For instance, Singer tried to build a business machines business for ten years but finally quit in 1975. The business was still unprofitable.

Second, I have continued to add business units to the data base after the dissertation was completed. The sample size is almost two-thirds again as large as it was in 1976. The descriptive statistics from these additional businesses remain similar to those reported here. Also, I have seen nothing to change the inferences and guidelines suggested. This statement is not to say that everything is the same—for example, some of the recent businesses have set larger market share goals. I cannot yet say whether these businesses represent a more aggressive type of entrant but I hope they do. One of my major conclusions is that the executives responsible for entry sought too low a share of the served market.

Since the time this study was completed, the topic of market strategy for business units (as opposed to corporate strategy or brand strategy) appears to have grown in importance. I think this trend has occurred as corporate executives realized that effective strategic planning comes from a more "bottom-up" approach than from a primarily "top-down" approach. Coincident with, and part of, this realization is another approach: effective strategic planning is primarily a line manager activity, not a staff activity.[1]

Perhaps the need for the involvement of all types of executives in strategic planning is nowhere seen more strongly than in decisions for new businesses. One of these decisions can be stated by asking, Which product-markets should we enter? Traditionally, the answer involves a corporate strategy decision. Another decision to be made is how we should enter them. Traditionally, this is more a functional level decision. Despite these differences the two decisions should not be made independently of each other. It is my hope that the conceptual framework and research findings presented here will help executives at all organizational levels to bring these two decisions together and improve the quality of new business decisions.

Many people helped me to complete the dissertation and my thanks are due to them all. Only a few can be acknowledged here. Professor Richard S. Rosenbloom, director of the doctoral program at the Harvard Business School at the time the dissertation was written, gave focus to my studies with his encouragement to pursue the combination of "disciplined knowledge and adminstrative practice." Professor Derek F. Abell, my dissertation chairman, spent countless hours with me helping to conceptualize entry in economics and strategy in marketing. His guidance throughout the thesis was invaluable. Professor Robert D. Buzzell, who exemplifies this combination in his own work, provided continual stimulation and challenge. Professor Jesse W. Markham first gave me the idea of combining parts of economics and marketing and then assisted me as I made the attempt. Although not on my committee, Professor Arthur Schleifer, Jr. helped me with

---

1. See, for instance, Peter Lorange and Richard F. Vancil, *Strategic Planning Systems* (Englewood Cliffs: Prentice-Hall, 1977), pp. xii–xv and 36–47.

statistical problems and the AQD data analysis package. I also wish to thank Professor Neil H. Borden, Jr. and all my professors in the MBA program at the Darden Graduate School of Business, University of Virginia: The MBA stage was an important step in preparing me for doctoral work.

When it came time to turn ideals and conceptualization into action, I received valuable support and counsel from Sidney Schoeffler, Ph.D. and Bradley Gale of The Strategic Planning Institute. This research could not have been completed without the pioneering work in the PIMS program. Mr. James Conlin, together with Ms. Barbara Benjamin and Mr. Stephen Land, provided great help with computer operations.

Although they must remain anonymous, I would like to thank the many managers who helped me to gather the data. It is only through their cooperation that research into business phenomena can occur. I hope that the results are adequate recompense for their investment of time and effort and sufficient encouragement to assist future research projects.

No project of this kind can take place without generous financial support. I am most grateful to Professor James P. Baughman and the Doctoral Program of the Harvard Business School, Professor Stephen A. Greyser and the Marketing Science Institute, Mead Johnson Corporation's doctoral fellowship, and the American Marketing Association for supplying the resources with which the original study was funded.

During the last twelve months in which I was turning the thesis into this book, I was again fortunate to receive support and encouragement from Dean Stewart Sheppard of the Darden Graduate School of Business, University of Virginia.

In preparing the book for publication, I received the assistance of several able people; in particular, I would like to thank Ms. Janet Marantz for editing the text and Ms. Nancy Hansen of the Division of Research for taking me through the seemingly endless publication tasks. Other valuable contributions were those of Ms. Libby Koponen, Joan Terrall, Thelma Prince, and Hilma Holton Gibb.

To Maylin, my wife, a special word of thanks is due. Although herself a student, as well as a wife and mother, she always found time to discuss my work and offer helpful comments. I am most grateful for her assistance and encouragement.

Finally, I accept responsibility for the study and the weaknesses it may contain.

Charlottesville, Virginia
May 1979

Contents

List of Tables

List of Figures

1. Introduction: Analyzing Corporate Diversification at the Business Unit Level

ENTRY BY ESTABLISHED FIRMS into product-markets where they have not previously competed interests both business administrators and economists. To business, entry into other markets represents diversification, an important source of future growth and profitability. Penrose (1959) points out that such diversification by established firms has enabled them to show continued growth over fifty or seventy-five years and more. For example, General Electric, in over eighty years, has moved from incandescent lamps alone to more than seven hundred product-markets, and their sales have risen from a miniscule level to $17.5 billion in 1977. Recent examples of entry by established firms include Gillette into felt-tip pens, IBM into copiers, John Deere into snowmobiles, and Texas Instruments into calculators, to name just a few.

In economic theory, entry plays a crucial role in attaining competitive markets. Economists have traditionally assigned this role to newborn firms, but are now realizing that it is also performed by established firms.[1] It has even

---

1. Hines (1957) noted that Alfred R. Oxenfeldt, *New Firms and Free Enterprise*, chap. 2; P. W. S. Andrews, *Manufacturing Business*, pp. 171–172; Corwin D. Edwards, *Maintaining Competition*, p. 188; Harold G. Vatter, "The Closure of Entry in the American Automobile Industry," *Oxford Economic Papers* (October 1952), p. 229; and R. B. Heflebower, "Toward a Theory of Industrial Markets and Prices," *American Economic Review* (May 1954), pp. 130–132; as

been argued that established firms can enter more easily and more effectively than can newborn firms. For example, P. W. S. Andrews (1959) pointed out that some of the problems faced by an entrant—such as acquiring capital, establishing a brand reputation, and attaining economies of scale—are less severe for established firms. He concluded, therefore, that "if the big business is important as a centre of economic power, it is also one of the sources of competition" (p. 172).

Hines (1957) added another advantage: "An established firm probably has unusually good knowledge of profit opportunities in markets contiguous to its own" (p. 135). Superior information, he argued, can enable an established firm to enter more rapidly and to require a smaller uncertainty allowance than the newborn firm. All these advantages led Hines to conclude that "there will be some cases in which new firms cannot enter at all, whereas established outside firms can" (p. 139). A practical example of such a case is provided by Brock (1975) in his study of the computer industry. He concluded: "The requirements for integrated systems business put entry out of the question for a new company. The only method of entry is through expansion from a profitable specialty base (as Digital Equipment is doing) or by subsidization of the computer effort from other activities of the corporation (as RCA and General Electric did before their withdrawal)" (p. 62).

Despite the importance of entry by established firms, little is known about the strategy and performance of the business units that made the entry. Scholars recognize that entrants' initial performance may not be profitable. For example, P. W. S. Andrews (1951) wrote:

> It would not be realistic to require that, on entry, they should be able to get normal profits. They will expect higher costs in the beginning than they will achieve

---

well as the literature on product diversification and multiproduct firms had recognized entry by established firms. Since then, Brunner (1961) has added some further thoughts; P. W. S. Andrews (1964) has pointed out that recognizing established firm entry means that "the differentiated segments of industries cease to be little monopolies but subject to strong competition of an oligopoly kind" (pp. 78–79); and Caves and Porter (1975) have developed this idea into "a general theory of the mobility of firms among segments of industry" (p. 2).

later as they get experienced, and will hope for increasing goodwill to enlarge their share of market. Their entry into the industry will be decided on the basis of estimates of what they can hope to achieve at some relatively more mature stage (p. 146).

But there is no cross-industry evidence on how long entrants have to wait, how much higher their initial costs are, or how long it takes them to enlarge their market share. The business trade literature has carried single-case "war stories" that indicate entry can be disastrous. NCR reported losses of $60 million in 1972, primarily because of entry into computers (*Business Week* 1973a). General Foods took a $39 million write-off in 1972 on its entry into fast-food chains (*Business Week* 1973b). Executives at ITT admitted that "ITT faltered now and then when it moved into unfamiliar industries" (*Business Week* 1973c).

Anecdotes do not, of course, provide a basis for understanding the experience of entrants in general. It is not known, for instance, how many entrant business units contribute only losses, and over what time period, to their parent companies. Nor can the performance of entrants be explained. This study is directed to this gap.

To answer the question, What has been the financial and market performance of the business units that made the entry? I describe statistically the experience of a sample of forty entrants. These statistics answer questions such as: What percentage of their costs did these entrants spend on marketing, research and development, and manufacturing in their early years? What was their investment intensity? What was their capacity utilization? What was their return on investment and cash flow–to–investment ratio? What market share had the entrants achieved after, say, two years and then four years? What was their cost position relative to the market's incumbents? What was their growth rate in sales revenues?

The second question dealt with here is, What markets were entered, what strategies were used, and with what influence on performance? I apply an analytical framework developed from business administration and economics to the descriptive statistics in an attempt to account for the observed performance. For example, I use the framework to define the strategies used by entrants and then to see how performance varied by type of strategy. Other aspects of the framework include the type of skill relatedness between the parent company and the entering business unit, the characteristics of the entered market, and the intensity of reaction from incumbents. Together, these factors serve to explain the variability in performance.

The antecedents of this research are many. Economists have studied the state of entry conditions (Bain 1956), the theory of limit pricing (Sylos 1962; Modigliani 1958), the extent of diversification (Gort 1962), the public policy implications of diversification (Edwards 1955; Markham 1973), the effect of entry on market structure (McGuckin 1972), and the determinants of entry (Orr 1974; Goercki 1975). Business researchers have studied the impact of entry on a firm's total performance (Rumelt 1974), the formulation of the firm's product-market mix (Ansoff 1965; Andrews 1971) and product line policy (Dean 1960; Kline 1955), the organizational processes involved in creating and managing new entrants (Bower 1972; Trevelyan 1974), and the evolution of multi-product-market firms (Scott 1970).

This past research has studied newborn entrants, the total firm, corporate strategy, broadly defined industries, or organizational process. But, newborn firms are not the only kind of entrants, total firms do not implement entry, corporate strategy is not business unit strategy, entry is not usually planned as entry into industries defined by SIC codes, and market processes are as likely to affect entrant performance as are organizational processes.

To illustrate: Bain (1956) studied entry conditions from the perspective of newborn firms. As P. W. S. Andrews (1964) commented, this definition of entry is restricted and "for this reason many of his conclusions are vitiated" (p. 79). Caves and Porter (1975) argued similarly, pointing out the need for a theory of entry that includes diversification by already existing firms: "the theory of entry barriers has been straitened by confining itself to the movement of firms from zero outputs [meaning new firms] to positive outputs" (p. 2).

Total firms, even established firms, do not implement strategy because once the decision to enter has been made, top management assigns responsibility for implementing the entry to a unit of the firm, variously referred to as a new venture group, a start-up business, a strategic business unit, a task force, a subsidiary, or a division. The entry experiences of this unit have not been studied previously.

Corporate strategy may tell the firm what it is offering, but it does not tell the business unit how it will compete for customers in its markets. Corporate strategy refers to the strategy of a firm as a whole, not to business unit market strategy. For example, the excellent studies of diversification by Wrigley (1970) and Rumelt (1974) specified the strategies of the whole firm in terms of the relatedness of diversification activities to the firm's main product.[2] This approach is most helpful in studying the performance of the whole firm and to the corporate strategist putting together a portfolio of product-markets. It is not as helpful to the strategist in charge of implementing the entry of a business unit into a chosen market. To understand entry from this perspective, we must focus on what the business unit offered to customers and how this compared with the preexisting competitors in that marketplace.

Top management usually does not think of entry into the two-, three-, or even four-digit SIC markets used in most economic research. A market to managers is defined by the producers whose behavior influences their own and by the products that are close substitutes for the same range of end uses. This concept, it might be noted, is much closer to the definition of a market in economic theory than to that used in much empirical work.[3] From the perspective of managers, SIC industries are often too broadly or too narrowly defined. The former results in a market

2. For example, a dominant-constrained strategy was defined as 70 percent of firm revenues in one product and 30 percent in closely related products; a related-constrained strategy had less than 70 percent of firm revenues in one product and the remainder in closely related products (see Rumelt 1974, chap. 1).

3. Stigler's understanding of the market in theory is, "individuals who together play the primary role in determining prices and quantities" (1952: 55).

consisting of products that are not close substitutes. The latter results in the exclusion from the market of products that are close substitutes. Either way, the competitive realities facing the entrant are distorted.

The organizational process leading to the creation of an entrant business unit by a large firm was well documented by Bower (1972) in that three of his four research cases involved the planning of new entries. Trevelyan (1974) picked up the organizational process in managing new businesses once launched. This focus on process emphasizes that new businesses have an internal, or organizational, constituency as well as an external, or market, constituency. Bower's and Trevelyan's research, among other contributions, helped in understanding the organizational process; it did not address the market conditions faced by new businesses.

This study builds on the research briefly summarized above. It attempts to extend previous research in that it deals with entry by established firms; it studies the performance of the business unit that made the entry; it examines the market strategy used; it studies the market that the managers specified as the one they were entering; and it focuses on the external influences rather than the organizational influences.

SOME SPECIAL DEFINITIONS

A number of terms used in this study are fairly common but are used here in a special sense. *Entry* has occurred when a firm already established in a line of business begins to compete in a product-market where it did not previously operate. Entry has not occurred when an existing product line is extended, as with capacity additions or new brand introductions by existing businesses. Entry has occurred if competitors already established in the entered market perceive the business as a new competitor and customers perceive the business as a new source of supply. Businesses started by acquisition are considered entrants only if they meet these criteria and the strategy and investment of the original business were substantially altered after acquisition. Joint ventures and businesses started under license are also considered entrants if they meet these criteria.[4]

The *market* that is entered is the meeting point of all those who are buying and supplying products that are close substitutes in the same range of end uses. Managers will define the relevant market on the basis of which producers influence their strategic decisions, and vice versa, and which customer groups producers appeal to. All the entered markets in this study's sample were oligopolies.

The unit that the firm organizes to effect entry is referred to as a start-up business or an entrant business. A *business* is defined as a unit of the parent company that has its own distinct product line; operates in a relatively self-contained market with its own competitors, technology, and economics; has its own budgets and estimates of income; and develops its own market strategy distinct from other units of the parent company.

A *start-up* or *entrant business* is, therefore, a business effecting entry, and its definition must meet the definitions of entry and business. Consequently, a start-up or entrant business is defined as a business that markets a product or service the parent company has not previously marketed; that requires the parent to obtain new commercial and operating knowledge; that requires adding new equipment, facilities, and people; that is recognized as a new competitor in the market; that results (either immediately or ultimately) in the establishment of an entity that meets the definition of a business given above; and that requires a significant investment of the parent company's resources to accomplish a result beyond the year in which the expenditure is made.

---

4. The definition of entry in the literature is ambiguous. Researchers have disagreed, in particular, on how to treat vertical integration, capacity additions, acquisitions, and new products. My definition is closest to Andrews (1949), who recognized entry by established firms and through vertical integration; to Needham (1969), in that capacity additions and new products are not recognized as entry but acquisitions are, provided that change more fundamental than the "mere change of ownership" (p. 98) occurred; to Bain (1968) on the treatment of capacity additions; but furthest from Bain (1956) who did not recognize entry by firms established in other markets.

Strategy is used to mean the competitive market strategies that are the entrant's answers to three questions: Who are we in this product-market, How will we attract customers, and What is the level and allocation of our efforts? Strategy here is distinguished from corporate strategy, which is more concerned with a different question, What business are we in, and with putting together a portfolio of businesses and product-markets.

Incumbents are the businesses already operating in the market prior to the arrival of the entrants under study. *Reaction* is the response of the incumbents to the new entry.

Performance is used to mean financial and market performance. Financial performance refers to measures such as return on investment, cash flow over investment, gross margin over sales revenues, and return on sales. Market performance refers to absolute and relative market share achieved. Because the entrants in this study's sample were still in their early years—the first four years of commercialization are reported—no inference is made that a certain kind of performance is "good" or "bad" or that some entrants have been "successes" or "failures." Rather, the thrust of this research is to establish what was their performance and then to establish how it came about.

At this juncture, it is worth emphasizing that I do not explore the question of why the parent companies entered. Although the answers to this question could have provided a measure of performance—Did the companies achieve their own reasons for entry?—it proved impractical to collect these data. One major problem was that the reasons for entry were not well articulated and rarely ever agreed upon by the managers involved.[5] Another problem was that several companies agreed to participate only if the nature of the entrant business and its product was not identified to the researcher. This condition prevented the detailed questioning necessary to identify what the parent company was trying to achieve. Finally, *ex post* research into *ex ante* intentions runs the risk of having the inten-

---

5. Philip A. Scheuble (1964) points out how objectives for new products can vary by departments within the same corporation (p. 111).

tions become close to the actual performance. Written
business plans provide one means of overcoming this risk,
but the first two problems mentioned above meant either
that they did not exist or that I was not permitted to examine them. Regretfully, therefore, the question why was
not studied.[6]

A NEW ANALYTICAL FRAMEWORK

There is no complete analytical framework for studying
entry, strategy, and performance; the researcher can therefore create his own. The framework developed for this
study consists of four basic concepts: relatedness, market
structure, entry strategy, and incumbent reaction. These
four concepts are shown in figure 1, together with a fifth
concept, entrant business organization, and one other input into strategy formulation, business goals. The latter
two, as explained above, are not covered in this research.
The four concepts used are interdependent, and collec-
tively, they influence performance.

Relatedness to the parent company refers to the likelihood that an entrant launched by an established company
inherits skills from the parent which it tries to transfer to
the entered market.[7] This idea can be found in the fields
of business policy, marketing, and economics. The policy
framework suggests that parent companies develop their
resources into a distinctive competence. Extensions in the
firm's activities should be related to this competence in
order to obtain satisfactory performance (K. Andrews
1971, chap. 3). Marketing captures a similar idea in the
concept *product-company fit*. New product introductions
are more likely to succeed, this concept suggests, if they

6. Considerable conceptualization and research into this question has already
been done. See, for example, Ansoff (1965, chap. 7); and Chandler (1962, chaps.
6–8).

7. The use of the word *relatedness* in this study should be distinguished from
its use by Rumelt (1974). *Relatedness* in Rumelt's work referred to the linkage
among *all* a firm's businesses, whereas here it refers to the linkage between *one*
business and the parent firm. Further, Rumelt expressed relatedness in terms of
the firm's dominant product, whereas here it is expressed in terms of skills
possessed by the executives of the parent firm.

FIGURE 1. ANALYTICAL FRAMEWORK FOR ANALYSIS OF ENTRANT
BUSINESS PERFORMANCE

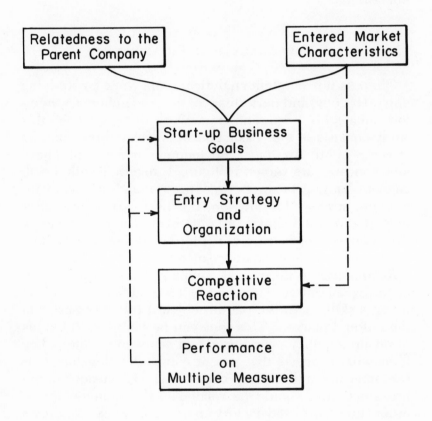

demand skills that managers already have. In economics,
a tangentially related concept is *marginal cost*; that is, the
marginal cost of using a firm's skills in new markets is low.
An additional concept in the same spirit is *organizational
slack* (Cyert and March 1963: 36–38); under some conditions, firms have excess resources and can, therefore, un-
dertake incremental activities.

The entrant business enters a market where it has not previously competed. Many fields suggest that performance is influenced by *market characteristics*. For example, the industrial organization paradigm of market structure–conduct–performance includes, under market structure, the number and relative size of competitors (Weiss 1971: 363–379), the growth rate (Gort 1962: 6–7), and so-called "barriers to entry," such as the extent of product differentiation and economies of scale (Bain 1956). Marketers emphasize the dynamic influence of market characteristics in the *product life cycle* concept. Both theoretical reasoning (Mickvitz 1959) and empirical research (Marketing Science Institute 1969) indicate that performance can vary according to the stage in the cycle. Finally, the marketing concept of *product-market fit* stresses the importance of a good match between product attributes and customer needs.

The *entry strategy* relates the skills of the entrant business to the customers in the market it has entered. A number of writers have emphasized the influence of strategy on performance. Foote (1966) wrote of each business's "positioning" itself in the market and developing a theme for its offering that is consistent with the chosen position; he cited "ease of use" (Kodak) and "reliability" (Zenith) as examples. Kotler (1972: 246) concluded, "The company's performance can vary tremendously, depending on its competitive strategy and style." The Profit Impact of Market Strategy (PIMS) Program has provided convincing evidence that relative product quality, relative price, and the interaction among product quality, marketing expenditures, and R&D expenditures are important influences on business profitability (Schoeffler, Buzzell, and Heany 1974).

Finally, entrants into oligopolies may provoke *reaction* from incumbents that prevents them from attaining the volume or price level needed to survive in their new market. Consider the position of the incumbents: they have an acceptable market share and are making satisfactory returns. Their position is now threatened by the entrant. They are likely to feel particularly threatened by established firm entrants because they know such entrants usually possess adequate resources—the parent can "cross-subsidize" the entrant business until it has reached a self-sustaining level of operations. If the incumbents decide to preserve their position, then they must react and match or better the entrant's offering. The resulting "war" (Marris 1968) is likely to raise the entrant's costs and lower its volume.

2. Specification of the Variables

THE FOUR CONCEPTS of the analytical framework—relatedness, entered market, entry strategy, and reaction—were refined into measurable variables on the basis of the literature and preliminary field research. The variables themselves are defined here, and their measurement is explained in the subsequent chapters devoted to each concept.

RELATEDNESS

There are two variables for the concept of the relatedness of the entrant to its parent: a classification of types of relatedness and an index of familiarity.

Types of Relatedness

A number of classifications exist to express the relatedness between a firm's existing and new activities. The scheme used by Rumelt was briefly discussed in chapter 1. Ansoff (1965) created a two-by-two box with present and new mission on the vertical and present and new products on the horizontal. The cell defined by new mission–new product represented diversification. He then constructed another box to expand the diversification cell into existing and new customers on one dimension and new products utilizing related technology and unrelated technology on the other. Some of the classificatory variables emerging from this box were marketing related and marketing and technology related (see also Ansoff 1957).

Vernon (1974) developed a classification to describe the relatedness among multinational firms' foreign expansion activities. The four types were exploitation of a technological lead, a strong trade name, advantages of scale, and a scanning capability.

The classification of types of relatedness to be used here is based on the identification of functional skills: technology, manufacturing, and marketing for example. Five types of relatedness have been isolated: technological, scale economy, marketing, vertical integration, and conglomerate. These five types are not necessarily mutually exclusive: the degree to which they overlap will be investigated empirically in chapter 7.

Technology Relatedness. Technology is a most likely basis for entry into other markets because corporate research often creates additional opportunities. Indeed, Gort (1962) found that companies with high technological skill (as measured by the ratio of technical to all employees) were the heaviest diversifiers, as measured by the number of two-digit SIC industries. Chandler (1962) and Rumelt (1974) have used the term *extensible technology* to describe this basis of entry. Extensible technology is one that involves skills that are not confined to a particular industry, material, or process. Rumelt notes, "This special property of extensibility was and still is a key influence on the ease with which a firm can diversify" (p. 133).

Firms with extensible technology are likely to uncover improvements of one kind or another that have potential outside the firm's primary activities. Chemical companies' stumbling onto graphite that is now used to make golf club shafts is an example. Furthermore, their skills can often be transferred to other products as contiguous technologies develop. One example is Hewlett-Packard's application of its scientific and engineering skill to entering the hand calculator market with a product for engineers. Another is provided by Bower (1972) in his description of one entry decision: "Once again, the basis for a major strategic decision was the existence of a capability rather than a well-studied choice of division or group management to enter fire protection" (pp. 184–185).

Scale Economy Relatedness. P. W. S. Andrews (1951: 168) points out that some manufacturing processes and equipment are sufficiently flexible to permit, with some modifications or extensions, entry into nearby markets. The sharing of existing facilities permits economies through higher plant utilization and lowers both the scale economy and absolute cost barriers to entry. One example is provided by Kimberly-Clark's entry into diapers with paper diapers. Brunner (1961) considers the entry of chemical companies into chlorine another example of this type. Kottke (1966: 30) notes that "the paper, textile and apparel industries are replete with examples."

Scale economies also arise from familiarity with the manufacturing methods used in the market to be entered. The learning time is shorter and start-up costs are reduced. For example, a rayon producer, used to a job-shop process, entered polyester, a bulk manufacturing process, and found itself at a disadvantage against chemical company entrants because they were more familiar with process production. Having related manufacturing experience can enable a later entrant to overcome the effect of experience on costs (Boston Consulting Group 1970). Using related experience means that the entrant can draw on an existing experience curve and achieve a lower starting position, and lower costs, on the new experience curve in the entered market. This experience transfer may lessen the entrant's cost disadvantages.

Marketing Relatedness. Some firms develop great expertise in marketing and make this the basis for their entry. The expertise could be in serving a certain type of customer (for example, the housewife), or in differentiating their products and segmenting their markets (Smith 1956), or in developing low-cost distribution and customer service systems, or in exploiting famous brand names and mass-media communication. An example of capitalization on some of these marketing skills is Gillette's entry into disposable lighters and felt-tip pens. Indeed, Gillette's claimed skill for planning their diversification activities is, "We can market any product that can be sold through mass merchandising outlets at $5 retail or less."[1] Another example is Xerox which has made an explicit decision to enter new markets by transferring their marketing skills (*Fortune*, May 1974). Their most recent entry into typewriters demonstrates their approach: *Business Week* (October 1974) commented, "Observers are more impressed with Xerox's marketing expertise than with the product it is introducing . . . Xerox has the marketing organization to sell lots of Model T's." An example of famous brand names to assist entry into new product-markets was provided by Hines (1957): "Hotpoint" attached to an entry into refrigerators and "Frigidaire" attached to an entry into stoves (p. 136).

Vertical Integration Relatedness. Vertical integration relatedness arises from a corporate strategy decision to add a stage of production or distribution to its own operations instead of using the open markets for that stage. The potential advantages of integration include lower costs through technological interdependencies, better distribution by supplementing existing distribution markets and higher value-added by assembling more of the end product, or, of course, assembling the end product in its entirety. A notable example of this kind of entrant is Texas Instruments' entering the marketing of hand calculators. TI integrated forward when it was already the world's largest supplier of integrated circuits. It used the savings achieved by integration to offer massive price cuts (according to *Electronic News*, January 1972, TI's entry price was $119 compared with Bowmar's $179) and a fuller line than existing firms. Later, TI was reported to be considering entry into the retailing of calculators in order to ensure customer servicing and a better match between their demand stimulation activities and the availability of their product.

Each stage added, either backward or forward, represents an entry into a market to which the established firm was previously a customer or a supplier. The business unit

---

1. Remarks by a Gillette group vice president at a class session of Harvard Business School Advanced Management Program, 1974. See also the case Gillette SRD 9-574-058.

making the integration move faces new customers. Likewise, former customers or suppliers now become competitors. Heflebower (1954) believes that entry by established firms into adjacent levels is widespread and likely to succeed, "both because of the awareness of entry possibilities which a vertically adjacent firm is likely to have and because such firms often possess the characteristic essential for successful entry" (pp. 130–131). Although Heflebower does not specify the characteristic, it may be presumed that he means knowledge of an important component, material, or process, which, as Kottke (1966) notes, may enable a business to design a product closer to the customers' wishes. The data in chapter 7 will help clarify this matter.

Conglomerate Relatedness. Much diversification activity has been built on a financial skill rather than a technology, manufacturing, or marketing skill. Entrant businesses with a conglomerate relatedness to their parent do not seek to transfer a functional skill to a new market. Rather, they enter a market because it shows attractive growth and the parent company has funds available for investment. Such entries may also be made to fill a blank spot in the established firm's portfolio of businesses (see, for example, Cox 1974). These entrants therefore exhibit little or no relatedness to the parent company's current technology, manufacturing, or marketing operations, nor to its products, but do draw on central managerial services and investment funds.

Index of Familiarity

A major problem faced by managers entering markets where they have not previously competed is their lack of familiarity with some or all the skills required in the entered market. For example, a successful hospital equipment company entered the hospital pharmacy market, where the managers faced new decision-makers. They had to learn new selling methods, meet different kinds of manufacturing standards, and extend their technological skills.

Field research has indicated that familiarity could be a most important influence on performance. At least, in the minds of managers, their new businesses have performed worst when they have had to learn the most. Rumelt (1974) investigated a similar hypothesis and established that high corporate performance was associated with a high degree of relatedness among diversification activities.

In this research, the key skills of interest are the functional skills of R & D, manufacturing, distribution, selling, and marketing as they are used in the market of entry. Managers rated their familiarity with these skills at the time the entry was made. The two relatedness variables cover the *type* of skill that was being transferred to the entered product-market and an assessment of parent company executives' familiarity with *all* the functional skills as they are practiced in the market of entry.

ENTERED MARKET

There are two variables describing the entered market: a classification combining its structure and stage of development and a continuous variable measuring its growth rate.

Type of Market

Several classifications and variables exist to describe market characteristics, both static and dynamic. Static characteristics on both the demand and the supply side include the number and relative size of sellers and buyers, the degree of product differentiation, the fixed cost to total cost ratio, and entry barriers such as economies of scale, existing customer loyalties, and absolute cost economies.[2]

The number of sellers already in the market affects entrants' probable performance because markets with fewer sellers are likely to be more difficult to enter. A small number means a heightened sense of rival interdependence: incumbents are more directly threatened by any

---

2. These variables are the traditional emphasis of industrial organization studies, see Bain (1968, chaps. 5–8), Scherer (1971, chaps. 1, 3, 4, 9, and 14), or Caves (1972) for a concise summary.

gains in output made by the entrant and, therefore, may react so as to hinder the entrant's progress.[3]

The relative size distribution of firms can be important because if incumbent businesses belong to parent companies that are larger than the parent company launching the entrant, they possess superior resources and can react to entry strongly. Furthermore, through cross-product subsidization,[4] they may be able to sustain a high level of reaction. Marris (1964), drawing from the two-person zero-sum game called gambler's ruin, states that the outcome of "conflict" between incumbents and entrant depends on the entrant's relative commercial advantage and relative resources. If the commercial advantage is neutral and the initial resources are unequal, "the chance of ultimate win for a given player is $1/(1 + r)$, where r is the ratio of opponent's initial resources to his own" (p. 194). A recent illustration of the influence of resources is the entry of Texas Instruments into calculators. Based on 1974 sales for TI and Bowmar, the value of r for TI was 1/12; in this example, the entrant had more resources than the leading incumbent. Assuming the commercial advantage was neutral, the gambler's ruin calculation means that TI's chances of winning were 0.92 and Bowmar's were 0.08.

Buyer concentration affects the level of margins in the entered market. A high concentration of buyers gives them stronger relative bargaining power than the entrant, which can result in the entrant's paying higher sales promotion costs and receiving lower margins.

Product differentiation refers to differences among products that are close substitutes for one another. Entrants into highly differentiated markets have to consider which particular niche of the market they wish to attack or

---

3. For example, the Sylos Postulate (Sylos 1962; Modigliani 1958) predicting output maintenance by incumbents and Stigler's (1966) suggestion of output increases. These, and other reactions, are explicitly discussed and tested in chapter 10.

4. Markham (1973) found very little evidence of cross-product subsidization in his study of 211 diversified manufacturing companies. The practice remains a possibility, however, and potential entrants would be well advised to consider its likelihood of occurrence.

whether they will offer a product to the mass market. Entrants into undifferentiated markets face no such decision but must decide whether they can gain a profitable share in a market of identical products and prices.

Product differentiation also appears as a possible barrier to entry: overcoming existing customer loyalties may raise costs for the entrant above the level of those incurred by the original incumbent firm.[5] Similarly, economies of scale may be a barrier because they raise the share of the market needed to be cost competitive (Bain 1956).

Many of these static aspects of markets are well summarized in the economic models of market structure. The oligopoly model deals with few firms, recognizes rivals' interdependence and the existence of entry barriers, and handles product differentiation by two submodels—differentiated oligopoly and undifferentiated, or pure, oligopoly. The monopolistic competition model deals with a large number of firms, all of which sell differentiated products that are close substitutes. Unfortunately, these models do not specify precisely the meaning of few and large. Also, they do not relate the number of firms to the amount of seller concentration.

Various attempts have been made to develop a more complete definition of the oligopoly structure. Bain (1968) identified five types of oligopoly based on four-firm seller concentration and whether a competitive fringe existed: his type 1a has four-firm seller concentration of 90 percent or more and no competitive fringe, and his type 5 has four-firm seller concentration of 25 percent or more and a strong competitive fringe (1968: 137–144). Kaysen and Turner identified two types: type 1 with an eight-firm concentration of 50 percent or more and type 2 with 33 percent or more (1959: 26–41). At this stage, it need only be noted that the procedures for refining the oligopoly model exist and these will be applied to this study's data in chapter 8.

The structure models do not capture the dynamic characteristics of markets. For this purpose, the product life

---

5. Plant and marketing costs incurred to get into business are not barrier costs; the additional costs for entrants refer to costs over and above start-up costs. In a sense, these additional costs are penalty costs for being a late entrant.

cycle model is more appropriate. This model divides market acceptance over time into four stages: introductory, growth, maturity, and decline. While clear dividing lines between stages are not suggested, the general notion is that the introductory stage is characterized by uncertain customer acceptance and methods of production; the growth stage is characterized by real annual growth of about 10 percent or more and by continuing evolution in production methods and number and size of competitors; the mature stage shows wide market acceptance and growth approximating total economy growth, and production methods and competitive structures are stable; and the decline stage is characterized by negative growth and exit by some competitors.

Empirical research (MSI 1969) has established the existence of these relationships. Generally, as products move through their introductory, growth, maturity, and decline stages, so sales, the number of customers and suppliers, the number of brands, and variety in manufacturing technologies and product features first increases and then decreases.

Mickwitz (1959) had observed these changes much earlier and set them up as assumptions from which he deduced the relative effectiveness of price, quality, services, packaging, and advertising. In the introductory stage, he reasoned, price and service have low sales elasticity, whereas improved quality and advertising have the most impact on sales. As products move from the growth stage into the mature stage, price-insensitive buyers are few and sellers try to expand total demand by lowering price to attract price-sensitive buyers. Advertising, quality, and service play a secondary role to price in the early mature stages. Through the mature stage, packaging becomes more important as rivals seek ways to differentiate a product that has become standardized. That is, there is little technological opportunity left with which to create physical differences, either in features or quality. Finally, markets move from maturity into decline, at which time total demand is once again insensitive to price, although individual business demand is highly sensitive to price, and marketing strategy has to try and find new applications.

The predominant message from the life cycle model is that markets change, as do buyer perceptions and characteristics, and these have a profound influence on the effectiveness of market strategies. Continuous market change means that certain strategies will be more appropriate in some stages of market development than in others. Furthermore, firms with certain skills will find it easier to enter during a certain stage than firms with other skills. Consequently, firms with, say, marketing skills might enter a market when the great wave of technological opportunity and primary demand expansion has passed, but end buyers are becoming conscious of brands, styles, and features, and immediate buyers are changing from specialty stores to convenience stores. The Gillette entry into felt-tip pens cited earlier provides one example. It is even possible that market change creates advantages for the entrant because he may see the market need for different skills before the incumbents do. The product life cycle, therefore, emphasizes that the essence of choosing an appropriate entry strategy is to get a good match between parent company skills and the entered market's stage of development.

Some economy in variables can be effected by combining these two models of markets. All products or services start their life with an innovator who is at first a monopolist. As customers become more familiar with the innovation and as manufacturer quality improves, the rate of adoption rises—the life cycle model calls this the growth stage. At this time, more businesses enter and the oligopoly structure may apply. If enough entrants come in, the structure will change to monopolistic competition and then, as maturity sets in, weaker competitors will exit and the market structure reverts to oligopoly. This combination of these two models is shown in figure 2.

This combination provides one classificatory variable which describes markets on both the demand and supply sides and captures some of their more important static and dynamic characteristics. The combination creates four stages of the life cycle and three market structures, which yields twelve different market types. The most likely of these into which entry might occur are:

FIGURE 2. MARKET MODELS AND THE PRODUCT LIFE CYCLE

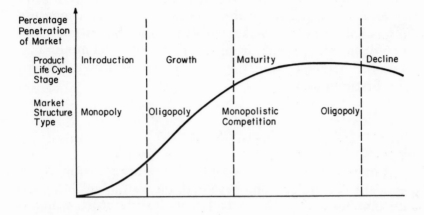

- Introductory monopoly
- Introductory oligopoly
- Growth oligopoly
- Growth monopolistic competition
- Mature oligopoly

It remains an empirical matter to assess the applicability of this classification of markets and this will be done in chapter 8.

Market Growth Rate

Although the product life cycle model is a proxy for, among other things, market growth, it seems advisable to explore this characteristic as a variable in its own right. First, it is a measure with wide acceptance and common understanding. Second, the influence of growth on many aspects of market evolution has already received much research attention.[6]

---

6. The literature is extensive but two examples are: Orr (1974) on growth as a determinant of entry; Kamerschen (1968) on the impact of growth on market concentration.

Growth in this study will always refer to the growth of the market that managers defined they were entering. Two different growth rates are relevant. The first is the preentry growth rate; that is, the average annual growth rate prior to entry for a period of three years. The second measure refers solely to the market growth while the entrant competed therein; that is, from the first year of commercialization. This measure is the average market growth rate for the first four years.

ENTRY STRATEGY[7]

A more extended review of the literature relevant to this concept is required before specifying variables. It should be emphasized at the outset that the literature contains discussion of many different dimensions of strategy, usually not in a precise and clear manner. Conceptualization, definition, and measurement of strategy is still at a low level of development. Indeed, Bain (1968) was driven to contend that "market conduct cannot be fully enough measured to permit us to establish a meaningful association between market conduct and performance" (p. 329). An indication of the undeveloped state is that a taxonomy, usually an early step in the study of a subject, is not generally agreed on by researchers in the field. Even the definition of terms varies enormously. This review of the literature first traces briefly the identification of strategy variables, then discusses a methodological problem, next presents some taxonomies of strategy, and finally discusses a new notion in the literature called *posture*. This review sets the background against which the variables used in this study will be defined.

Economists' studies of strategy have concentrated on output and price. Various concepts have been devised to describe price strategies, ranging from outright price fixing

---

7. Special acknowledgment and thanks should be made here to several discussants on conceptualizing market strategy: Professors Derek Abell, Joseph Bower, Robert Buzzell, Richard Caves, Jesse Markham, and Michael Porter of Harvard University.

to price leadership (Markham 1951). Chamberlin (1932) added quality and sales promotion outlays as additional strategic variables but these have not been widely studied by economists. Aspects of product policy such as styling (Menge 1962), obsolescence (for example, Brock 1975) and brand proliferation (Lanzillotti 1954—"self-competing products" in his terminology) have also received attention in economists' study of strategy.

In the marketing literature, writers have given attention to a wider array of variables and to the interaction among them. The marketing mix (Borden 1964) explicitly emphasized the interaction of eleven elements and conceptualized the marketing manager as a "mixer of ingredients."[8] The eleven elements are product planning (the market segments to be served and the product lines to be offered), pricing, branding, channels of distribution, personal selling, advertising, promotions, packaging, display, servicing, and physical handling.

The methodological problem arises from the interactions among these variables. Marketing theory stresses that satisfactory performance comes from an internally consistent mix. Yet, to handle the relationships among so many variables, with the effectiveness of each depending on the levels of the others, is an extremely complex task.

This methodological problem can be tackled by two different research approaches. One is to focus on each dimension individually, a simple approach. Alternatively, interaction among the various dimensions can be recognized and attempts made to identify internally consistent strategies, a more difficult approach.

For example, Bain (1968) takes the first approach and suggests that each firm set its preferred levels on the variables of price, output, sales promotion outlays, and quality and then have these levels adjusted either through rivalry or through collusion. By taking each variable in turn, it becomes possible to specify some strategies for each (chap. 9).

Although this first approach conflicts with marketing the-

---

8. Attributed to James W. Culliton, *The Management of Marketing Costs* (Boston: Harvard Business School, Division of Research, 1948) by Borden.

ory, examples of the second approach are rare. Consequently, general principles on what mix is internally consistent and under what conditions have not been fully specified. Internal consistency remains a largely situational concept. The current state of development is a collection of taxonomies, some of which are briefly reviewed below.

An early example was W. R. Smith's (1956) twofold classification of marketing strategies into either product differentiation or market segmentation. A product differentiation strategy described sellers with a product orientation, rather than a consumer orientation, whose approach was to build some difference into the product and then advertise it heavily as suitable for the mass market. The opposite strategy is market segmentation, defined as sellers who, recognizing consumer heterogeneity, divided consumers into groups with common needs and then designed a version of the basic product suitable for each group.

Kotler (1972) has classified strategies into those suitable for the dominant firm in an industry and those suitable for the smaller firms. Kotler argues that smaller firms should concentrate on improving their relative position by differentiating themselves from the larger firms. He suggests four different strategies: improving the product, finding a different segment of the market, opening up a new channel of distribution, or developing a superior advertising campaign. Other possibilities are innovation in personal selling, packaging, pricing, services, and promotion (pp. 257–260). In contrast, the larger firms' objective is to "discourage" or "discipline" the smaller firms. Their strategy alternatives are innovation, fortification (brand proliferation so as to close smaller firms out of the market), confrontation (price war), and persecution (using their relationships with suppliers, channels, and legislators to restrict smaller firms) (pp. 260–263).

Porter (1975) has suggested that in convenience consumer goods, it is possible to identify two prototypical marketing strategies: differentiated product and nondifferentiated product (private label brands and local brands) (chap. 7). Sellers following a differentiated strategy are likely to use most, if not all, of the elements specified by Borden in an attempt to create customer loyalty to their brand. Nondifferentiated sellers, however, produce to a reseller's product specification (for example, a retail chain) and rely primarily on low price to obtain a share of the market. Industries where these two strategies occur include orange juice (Minute Maid and A&P private label), canned vegetables, and soups.

A similar but more general taxonomy has emerged from the experience curve (Boston Consulting Group 1970) and its application to strategy: cost reduction versus defensible segmentation. A cost-reduction strategy seeks the greatest accumulated volume with the objective of attaining the best cost position relative to competitors. A defensible segmentation strategy seeks a portion of the market which the holder can defend against larger competitors, in spite of their superior cost position.

The final point to be mentioned here from both the economics and marketing literature is a concept variously referred to as "market position" (Heflebower 1954) or "posture" (Foote 1972). Writers using these terms seem to have in mind something in addition to the marketing mix elements already discussed. An early reference to market position was Heflebower (1954), who explained it as: "By market position is meant more than what the firm sells and to whom and by what means, and more than its share of the volume. Instead, market position is that composite of attributes which governs the ability of the firm to compete" (p. 125). The "composite of attributes" was not elaborated, but, judging by later comments, it appears to refer to more enduring characteristics of rivals, such as their skills, goodwill, or reputation, and the way in which they have typically competed. That is, the marketing mix creates something larger than the sum of its parts which gives some distinctiveness to a business, and this, in turn, provides them with a niche in the market. Heflebower further argues that each business in a market has a "market position," and this explains the stability of markets and the absence of price competition (as opposed to the usual explanation of collusion).

Foote (1972) has a similar view: each rival in an industry applies its distinctive competence[9] to satisfying the needs of a particular customer segment, rather than competing head-on with petty product differences, price cuts, and ever escalating advertising. This distinctive competence eventually becomes a theme that guides the strategic decisions of a business (such as Kodak's "ease of use," cited above in chapter 1). This theme is the "hallmark" or "posture" of a business by which it is recognized by consumers and rivals.

Levitt (1962) has talked about the posture of a business in respect to whether it typically tries to innovate, a "leader," or whether it is typically a "follower."

Kotler (1972) has distinguished between market strategies and marketing strategies. According to him, the purpose of market strategy is "to ensure that the firm achieves an adequate share in each market in which it chooses to participate" (p. 230). There is a suggestion of position here, a certain level of market share. Marketing strategy is defined as guiding the "level, mix and allocation of marketing effort over time" (p. 46). *Effort* as used by Kotler refers to price, product, promotion, distribution, and service.

A notion similar to market position or posture also occurs in the industrial organization literature. For example, the optimal size of production scale chosen by a business is considered a major decision—for an entrant, the sole decision.[10] Although stating it as the sole decision is too strong, it is certainly a decision with enormous bearing on the eventual position or share achieved. Another variable that is discussed is the integration of a business relative to rivals. Greater relative integration, it is argued, can give a business competitive advantages (for example, Caves 1972: 51).

It seems generally agreed in the literature that posture and mix decisions are related. Indeed, to some (Heflebower and Foote above) posture seems to be the long-term result of successive marketing mixes. Others (such as Kot-

---

9. Originally used by Philip Selznick in a similar sense in *Leadership in Administration* (New York: Harper and Row, 1957).

10. See Caves and Porter (1975: 4).

ler above) have argued normatively that posture decisions precede mix decisions. For example, Abell (1975) has suggested that whether to use a skim or penetration price (a mix decision) is also a choice about how broad or narrow a market entry to make (a posture decision). It is preferable, Abell argues, to make the breadth of entry decision first because that defines the segment and its needs that will be served. In turn, all other functional policies (such as marketing mix, manufacturing, and organization) should be designed to serve this segment and its needs (p. 3).

The order of the relationship between posture and mix in practice is not clear-cut: the interaction that exists within the mix would also seem to exist between posture and mix. For example, a strategist could decide on a skim price because he wishes to maximize short-term profits by taking advantage of any inelasticity that may exist. From a skim price, he works back to a small market share and, therefore, a narrow entry. Alternatively, he could identify a segment that is inelastic with respect to price first, and then make a decision to charge a skim price.

The primacy of these two concepts is not investigated in this study; rather, the research recognizes the recent development of posture variables in the literature and examines the influence on performance of a selection of these, as well as of some marketing mix variables.

This brief review of the literature has indicated several points that needed to be borne in mind in planning this research. First, entry strategy has two components, posture and marketing mix. Second, an approach is needed that handles the methodological problem of interactions among strategy variables. Third, some existing classification schemes can be drawn upon for creating a classification of entry mixes.

Accordingly, posture variables are investigated separately and are defined in this study as the degree of innovation offered by entrants relative to incumbents, the degree of forward and backward integration relative to incumbents, and the size of production entry scale. These variables seem to be the most specific in the various discussions of posture, they add some strategic characteristics not included in the mix, and data for them can be collected.

The definition of marketing mix elements used here is Borden's (given above) because it is commonly accepted and understood in the marketing literature. However, not all his elements are investigated. The mix variables that are investigated here are price, quality, length of product line, breadth of segment served, distribution, services and expenditures on the sales force, advertising, and promotion, all relative to incumbents.

With reference to the methodological problem presented by interaction among variables, the approach here was to assume it exists but to collect disaggregated data so that its existence could be empirically explored. That is, data were collected on all the variables individually, and aggregation of variables into types of strategies was attempted with the data already at hand.

Classification of Entry Strategies

The tentative classification of entry strategies based on marketing mix variables that guided the subsequent empirical exploration is presented here.

Starting at the simplest level, observe the market demand curve in figure 3, first in the price elastic region with price P_1 at which the incumbents supply Q_1. The entrant's demand curve is that part of the market demand curve beyond Q_1, moved to the price axis to indicate the entrant is starting from zero output.[11] As shown by P_1C, the entrant can attempt to gain output by cutting price to a level below P_1 or by attempting to move its demand curve to the right toward ER. The price cut has to be bigger, the more inelastic the market demand curve; that is, the more incumbents have succeeded in differentiating the market. Moving to the inelastic region, the incumbents supply Q_2 at price P_2. The price-cutting strategy is not attractive because the elasticity is now less than one; the entrant must rely on moving its demand curve to the right in order to obtain a share of the market.

This analysis identifies two strategies: one is for the entrant to be a price cutter; the other is to move the en-

---

11. See Modigliani (1958) and Needham (1969).

FIGURE 3. Demand Curve Facing a Potential Entrant

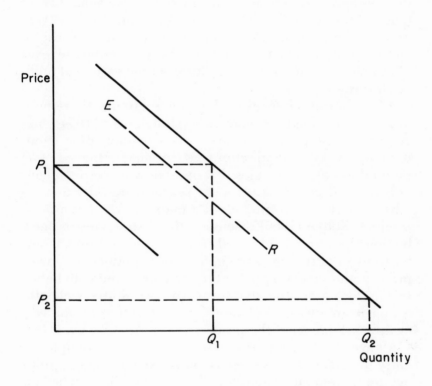

trant's demand curve to the right. But this latter strategy
is too general because managers can attempt it in several
different ways. As has been seen, the variables under their
influence, in addition to price, are product, quality, promotion, services such as warranties and credit, and choice
of market segments. In addition, by dropping the assumption of no intermediate distribution stages implicit in figure 3, an additional variable is obtained, distribution meth-

ods. By dropping another assumption implicit in figure 3, that market demand curves are static, businesses can consider additional strategies of exploiting or fostering market growth. Exploiting growth means that entrants could enter markets in a largely imitative way in the expectation that they will be carried along by market expansion: Marris (1968) has termed this "bandwaggoning." Fostering growth might entail a nonimitative entry, through use of all the variables so far mentioned, plus increasing the level of promotion or service expenditures or the variety of product forms.

A number of other researchers have discussed the nonimitative use of these variables. Heflebower (1954) suggested at least three strategies: market segmentation, product improvement, and improved services. Hines (1957) pointed to entry strategies that open new marketing channels, extend geographical areas served, and offer a specialized, high-priced product or a mass market, low-priced product. Kottke (1966) discussed three strategies of entry by what he termed "classical competition": offering a better product at the same price, the same product at a lower price, or the same product at the same price but with better service or more attractive terms (p. 28). Kottke's classification is an attempt to handle the interaction among two or three elements of the mix.

Alemson (1969), describing some Australian examples of entry, noted strategies such as market segmentation, product improvement, extending the product line—what he called "spreading the assortment"—and increased marketing expenditures. Bevan (1974) provided a helpful account of the entry of Golden Wonder (Imperial Tobacco Co., U.K.) into the British potato crisp market, (Smith's was the major existing firm in the market):

> The licensed premises were Smith's main market in 1960, and it seems that when Golden Wonder planned their expansion into England a decision was made not to compete with Smith's in that market. Clearly, Golden Wonder was aware that the crisp market could be segmented into three major groups: men, purchasing crisps in licensed premises; women, buying crisps in grocer

shops for domestic consumption; and teenagers and children, consuming crisps as light snacks during the day.

Of these three segments, the latter two had remained quite undeveloped during the 1950's. It was particularly to the second segment—the housewife—that Golden Wonder's advertising and sales campaigns in 1960–65 were aimed. Not only did their advertising (especially in television commercials) promote the image of crisps as a nourishing snack food, but also their sales force put most of their effort into ensuring that grocers, in particular, stocked crisps. The success of this new entry strategy—that is, identifying an undeveloped segment of the market, and concentrating most of the firm's marketing effort on it—was the main cause of the substantial growth of the market during the 1960's (p. 293).

The Golden Wonder entry points not only to market segmentation but also to innovation in distribution (and to the need for a marketing mix to be internally consistent).

Kotler's classification of strategies mentioned earlier for the smaller firms is applicable to entrants because they too are trying to improve their relative position.

Drawing from this discussion, a classification of entry strategies based on individual marketing mix elements is:

• Price cutter
• Improved quality
• Broader or specialist product line
• Broader or narrower segment
• Improved services
• Distribution innovator

This classification guided initial analysis of the data. Thereafter, factor analysis on all of the marketing mix variables was used in an attempt to identify types of entry strategy. Finally, Kottke's idea of combining price and quality was investigated and a classification of price-quality combinations derived from the data.

The results of these empirical attempts at classifying entry mixes are shown in chapter 9. This chapter also shows the distribution of the sample on the posture variables mentioned earlier. Thereafter, chapter 9 presents data on the influence of these posture and mix variables on entrant business performance.

REACTION STRATEGY

The discussion here need only be brief because incumbents can react by changing exactly the same variables as were discussed in the previous section on entry strategy. Oligopoly theorists have almost entirely overlooked this fact, concentrating on the price-output reaction of existing firms (see Sylos 1962; Modigliani 1958; Stigler 1966; and Wenders 1971). According to Alemson (1970), reaction to entry in his Australian consumer goods sample rarely included price; the most frequent reaction was increased selling effort. A common form of this reaction was brand proliferation: in the case of cigarettes, he discovered that in ten years of bitter competition between the original monopolist and an entrant, the number of cigarette brands increased from 5 to 128. Bevan's account of entry into the British potato crisp market shows that when the incumbent reacted, it was with a change in marketing mix, mainly an imitation of the entrant's strategy.

The variables on which reaction is measured are price, capacity, product, marketing expenditures, and distribution. Reaction on these variables is measured individually and then they are combined into an index of reaction.

PERFORMANCE

There is no commonly accepted list of performance variables or method by which entrant businesses should be evaluated. In thinking of appropriate variables, one approach is to compare subsequent performance against planned performance. However, as noted in chapter 1, this approach was not practical in this research. Another method would be to evaluate whether the entrant business, at the margin, raised the performance typically shown by its parent. This method was also not practical because the businesses are still in a development stage.

An important objective of this research is to establish the performance of entrant businesses in their early years of operations. Consequently, there is a good case for taking common financial measures at different time periods and seeing what their values were. This information would provide some "benchmarks" against which future entrants could be evaluated. Three of these financial performance variables were selected. One is return on investment (ROI) because this variable enjoys common currency and is used in the PIMS analysis. Thus, comparisons of ROI performance can be made between entrant businesses and established businesses in the PIMS data base. Another variable is cash flow over investment because this is a measure of cash recovery. Finally, return on sales (net income–to–sales revenue ratio) is used to provide a sales revenue–based measure. Occasionally, performance on gross margin over sales revenues and cash flow over sales revenues is also presented.

Evidence from the Profit Impact of Market Strategy program (Buzzell, Gale, and Sultan 1975) and the Boston Consulting Group (1970) suggests that relative market share is an important determinant of return on investment. Given this relationship, it is apparent that an entrant should be trying to obtain a strong relative market share. Another performance variable, therefore, is the ratio of the entrant's share to the combined share of its top three competitors.

Another important aspect of performance is the cost position of the entrant relative to the incumbent (see, for example, P. W. S. Andrews 1964: 80; Needham 1969, chap. 7). If, after some period of start-up losses, the entrant business cannot obtain cost parity or a better cost position, then its eventual survival must be questionable.[12] Related to cost position is the entrant's level of prices. Failure to obtain parity or a better relative price-cost position must also lower the chances of survival. One performance variable is, therefore, the price–to–direct cost ratio[13] of entrants, judged relative to incumbents.

---

12. As Markham (1973) has pointed out, even large, diversified firms have a low tolerance of poor performing businesses.

13. Although treated as a performance variable here, it is recognized that this ratio can also be a measure of strategy.

The above discussion means that four performance variables are continuously used in this research: three are financial: ROI, cash flow over investment, and return on sales; one is a market performance variable, relative market share. Occasionally, a fifth variable is presented which combines the relative cost position (reflecting the efficiency of the entrant's operations) and the relative price position (reflecting the entrant's ability to obtain a price for its offering in the marketplace). The exact construction of these variables is shown in table 1.

The variables for each of the concepts have now been specified. These are summarized in figure 4, which shows

TABLE 1. CONSTRUCTION OF PERFORMANCE VARIABLES

$$\text{Pretax return on investment} = \frac{\text{Net pretax income}}{\text{Average investment}}$$

Income is calculated after deduction of corporate expenses but prior to interest charges. Investment is calculated as working capital plus fixed capital (valued at net book value).

Capitalized return on investment = above adjusted by capitalizing 100% of R&D expenses in all years; 100% of marketing expenses in first two years, and 50% thereafter depreciated at a rate of 10% per year.

Cash flow/investment = net income times one-half minus all investment in year 1 and incremental working capital and net investment in plant and equipment in years $t+1$ as a percentage of average investment.

Pretax return on sales = net pretax income as a percentage of sales and lease revenues.

Relative share = share of entrant as a percentage of top three competitors combined.

Relative price/cost = ratio of management's judgments on their selling price relative to incumbents' and judgments of their direct costs relative to incumbents'.

Gross margin/sales = sales revenues minus purchases, manufacturing, and depreciation as a percentage of sales and lease revenues.

Cash flow/sales = cash flow as defined above as a percentage of sales and lease revenues.

FIGURE 4. ANALYTICAL FRAMEWORK FOR STUDYING PERFORMANCE OF ENTRANTS LAUNCHED BY ESTABLISHED FIRMS: CONCEPTS AND VARIABLES

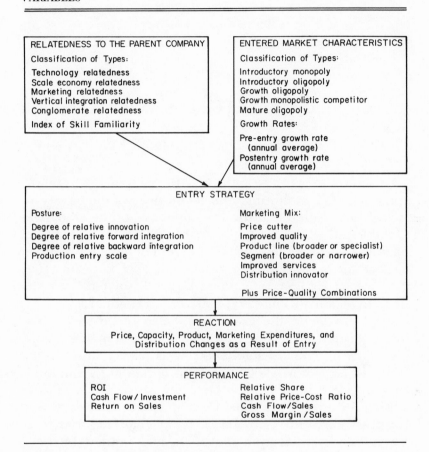

the analytical framework from chapter 1 with the relevant variables assigned to each concept.

3. Research Procedures

THIS CHAPTER IS CONCERNED with the sample, research approach, data gathering, and techniques of data analysis. It will be recalled that the first objective of the study was to put together a data base to enable description of entrant business performance, and the second objective was to try to account for variation in performance. I hope to move the current state of knowledge beyond isolated "war stories" to establish some "typical" or "average" results.

First, however, the groundwork had to be laid. Thus, the first stage of the research was a qualitative one involving visits to twenty established firms participating in the Profit Impact of Market Strategy program of the Strategic Planning Institute (SPI)—a nonprofit organization of companies interested in business strategy. I interviewed twenty-six executives, each of whom had experience in corporate diversification decisions and entrant business operations. The goals of this stage of the research were threefold: To test and refine the analytical framework, to agree on definitions and specify variables which influenced performance and for which data existed, and to recruit examples of entrant businesses for the sample. A follow-up visit tested the questionnaire.

SAMPLE

I recruited the sample of entrant businesses over a fifteen-month period from the twenty SPI companies that participated in the first stage. These companies share certain characteristics which should be borne in mind. First, all but one are in the *Fortune* top 200. Second, all are highly diversified and have frequently made entries into product-markets where they had not previously competed. Third, all share a great interest in the quantitative analysis of business strategy. Any company can join SPI and, therefore, those that have presumably differ in some systematic way from those that have not, say, the other firms in the *Fortune* 500. It is possible that this difference is associated with their great diversity and enhanced interest in strategic insights that are not industry-specific.

Certain characteristics about the entrant businesses should also be borne in mind. First, they are all survivors. The original sample design called for both entrants that had failed as well as entrants currently in commercialization. However, it turned out that managers had insufficient interest in dead businesses and the needed data could not be collected. Consequently, this sample of entrants is a group of survivors.

Second, not all the SPI companies submitted entrant businesses to the sample. Thus, there is some response bias within the SPI companies. Again, this bias may be tied to managers' interests in strategy because the companies that provided entrant examples were, mainly, the charter members of the PIMS program. No detectable bias seems to exist in terms of industry. The parent companies participate in a cross-section of industries: petroleum, chemicals, textiles, electronics, food, instruments and controls, machine tools, paper, and rubber. These companies may be described as very active participants in the PIMS program: some have as many as 30 or 40 businesses in the main PIMS data base of 600 businesses, and the PIMS reports are a routine feature of their strategic planning processes.

Third, the entrant businesses submitted are believed to be typical examples of the kinds of entrants regularly launched by their parent companies. The criteria for choosing which entrants to submit included: data availability; management interest in participating in this research project; top management interest in the business that was to be submitted; and entrant business age of at least two years. Although one or another of these criteria could distort the type of entrants submitted (for example, only those with their own accounting information), the PIMS representatives believe that the businesses are not unusual cases of their corporations' diversification activity.

There resulted forty entrant businesses with at least two years of data; twenty-eight of these also have data for their second two years of commercialization. The sample is analyzed by number of years of commercialization, rather than by calendar years. Thus, data are presented for the first two years and the second two years of commercialization. This procedure was followed because the research topic is strategy and performance of entrants from the year of entry; that is, the year of initial commercialization. In terms of calendar years, the sample embraces the late 1960s and early 1970s, a period which, as it happens, includes several different macroeconomic conditions. Such differences help the research because they mean that the results are less influenced by the macro environment prevailing at the time of entry.

The composition of the sample by type of business is shown in table 2. Clearly, industrial goods businesses dominate the sample. A more specific identification of the entrants is not possible because contributors submitted data on the condition that their identity, and that of their businesses, would not be disclosed. Furthermore, no data were submitted about the specific types of goods or services marketed by about 60 percent of the entrants. SIC numbers are not presented because, for reasons already

TABLE 2. SAMPLE COMPOSITION BY TYPE OF BUSINESS,
FIRST TWO YEARS OF ENTRY

Type of Business	Number	Percent
Consumer goods	6	15
Capital goods	7	18
Materials	7	18
Components	11	27
Supplies/other consumables	6	15
Services	3	7
Total	40	100

explained in chapter 1, they are of little value for studying entry; in any event, more than half the entrants refused to provide their SIC numbers. It is apparent, however, from conversations with the PIMS representatives, that most of the two-digit SIC industries listed under manufacturing are represented in the sample. It also seems a fair comment to add that the food (SIC 20), textiles (SIC 22), chemical (SIC 28), machinery (SIC 35), electric and electronic (SIC 36), and instruments (SIC 38) manufacturing industries have more than one entrant business in the sample, but that none has more than five.

With this description of the sample laid out, it is now appropriate to consider to what population the results reported here can be generalized. Ideally, one would like a population of all entrant businesses launched by established firms in the late 1960s and early 1970s. A sample could then be drawn from this population and the results held to be representative of it. Obviously, this sample of entrants does not meet this condition—first, because the population is nowhere defined and, second, because the sample is self-selected.

The population from which this sample is drawn can be summarized as a subset of the *Fortune* 200 that share the features of a high degree of diversification and whose managers are very interested in strategic planning. The businesses submitted are apparently typical examples of the kinds of entries regularly launched by this subset of established firms. There seems to be a good basis for believing that the sample is representative of this more restricted population of firms. That is, the first two years and second two years of commercialization shown here are what might be expected if data were obtained on the $n + 1$ entrant launched by a member of this restricted population. More caution is needed in interpreting these results for less diversified members of the *Fortune* top 200, the *Fortune* 201–1000, and entrant businesses launched by individuals.

RESEARCH APPROACH

Once the variables influencing a subject of inquiry have been identified, the next step is to measure the degree of their influence. For example, some of the interviewed executives suggested a number of variables that, in their experience, had affected the performance of one entrant business or another. However, they could not say whether the variables applied to all entrant businesses, to what degree they influenced performance, or how that influence varied under different conditions. This step is the quantitative stage of research and, in this study, it has been attempted by using a structural cross-sectional approach.

This approach is based on the proposition that there are general characteristics about businesses that cut across industry lines and business lines. That is, it is not necessary to know the specifics of an industry's manufacturing process, the physical composition of its products, its organizational structure, or the personal values of its managers in order to explain variation in business performance. Rather, it is sufficient to study those structural characteristics common to all businesses, such as their market growth rate, their relative competitive position, and their investment intensity, to name just a few. The variables identified in chapter 2 are examples of structural variables that are likely to be common to all entrant businesses and that can be expressed in quantitative terms, thus permitting the collection of a sample large enough for making generalizations about business performance.

These structural variables were analyzed cross-sectionally. The hypothesis behind this methodology is that variation in a dependent variable, in this case entrant business performance, is partially attributable to the differences in the values of the structural variables. In a sense, cross-section analysis can be regarded as a substitute for conducting an experiment—a method obviously precluded to strategy researchers. Each entrant business, therefore, is an experiment in entering a market. When enough of these "experiments" have been collected, research can begin to identify the relative importance of the structural variables, under different conditions. In other words, cross-sectional analysis offers the strategy researcher a methodology similar to that used in the physical sciences. Dr. Sidney Schoeffler of SPI calls this approach a search for "the laws of the marketplace." One indication of its value is that the PIMS model accounts for 84 percent of the variation in business unit return on investment (Schoeffler et al. 1974).

This study was not able to reap all the benefits of the cross-sectional approach because of the small sample size. Answering the question, What kind of entry strategy, in what kind of markets, with what kind of parent company relatedness, against what kind of incumbent, is likely to succeed? remains a long-term goal. Here, the focus is on describing entrant business performance and then generating some insights that help in understanding the performance by studying the variables one at a time. Thus, this research is a tentative first step in the field. It is expected, however, that the results should contribute to further development of theory about the interactive relationships among strategy, markets, firms, and businesses.

The study describes performance of this sample of entrant businesses in chapters 4, 5, and 6 and the structural, cross-sectional approach is used in chapters 7, 8, 9, and 10 in an attempt to understand variation in performance.

The data for chapters 4–10 were collected through three data forms:

- Data Form 1: Description of the business: products and services, customers, company relationships
- Data Form 2: Preentry expenses and postentry operating results and balance sheet information
- Data Form 3: Industry, market, and competition; entry strategy and competitive response

The data forms were completed by the managers of the entrant businesses. On average, about two person-weeks was required to obtain all the data. Most of the statistical and financial data were disguised by the parent company submitting the entrant business. Neither I nor the officers of SPI know the disguise factors used by any parent company.

Three sources of guidance were available to managers

providing the data. First, each received a Data Manual[1] used to guide data collection for the PIMS project. This manual defined terms, suggested solutions to the most frequent queries raised in previous data-gathering experiences, and expanded on some of the questions in the data forms. In addition, a separate manual, "What is a start-up business?" was provided which dealt with terms and questions specific to entrant businesses.

Second, each parent company has appointed an executive to be their PIMS representative. These executives were familiar with the project and guided managers on data preparation. Third, the author was available throughout the data-gathering period for further consultation. About half the forty entrant businesses raised questions with me.

Once the data forms were received, each was checked individually for arithmetical or logic errors. For example, Did sales revenue minus expenses equal the net income as shown? Did sales revenue divided by total market sales equal the market share as shown? A logic error could arise from conflicting answers to two questions. For example, in answer to the question about timing of entry, one answer could be a "later entrant into a more established market." In answer to the question about stage of product life cycle, the reply "introductory stage" would be in conflict with the answer to the timing question. When errors, actual or potential, were detected, I contacted the PIMS representative in the parent company concerned who, in turn, checked the data with the managers responsible for the business. After checking, the data for each business were key-punched which, in turn, was also checked. Finally, the data were entered into the data base.

Although some data errors may have slipped through this screening process, it seems likely that they are random errors. At the same time, this data base is likely to be much more accurate than any data gained from public sources about entry. For example, the definition of the market that was entered is more precise than the definitions used by the SIC. Furthermore, the financial data on the perform-

---

1. PIMS Phase III Data Manual, 1974.

ance of individual entrants are simply not available through public sources. Another advantage of these data is that they cover many different types of businesses; the results from this study are *not* confined to a particular industry.

DATA ANALYSIS

The first point that must be made about the data is that most of the continuous variables are distinctly nonnormally distributed. The variability around mean estimates is, in some cases, enormous. Some reduction in this variability was achieved by combining two years of data and taking the average: thus, the data are aggregated into the first two years and the second two years of entry. Nevertheless, the variability is still significant and, at one time, it was thought advisable to analyze the medians only. While this procedure provides a safeguard against being misled by outliers, it does not, of course, permit any kind of statistical inference. The final decision was to present both medians and means, test the means for significant differences, and present the results in a spirit of providing some rough guidelines. At all times, the medians were referred to before making a suggested conclusion: if the means went in one direction and the medians in another, then either the median direction was adopted or the data were regarded as uninterpretable.

The descriptive statistics of this sample of entrants are presented in chapters 4, 5 and 6, where data on preentry performance are also shown. Next, the ratios recorded by this sample in the first two years and the second two years of commercialization are compared with a subsample of the main PIMS data base. This subsample contains data for businesses in their fifth to eighth years of commercialization. The combination of this study sample and the PIMS subsample means that description statistics on the first eight years of commercialization can be presented.

Explanation of the performance of the study sample over the first four years is conducted in chapters 7, 8, 9, and 10. The explanation is attempted through cross-tabulation analysis of one independent variable at a time instead of

the multivariate techniques that the topic actually de-
mands. Several reasons favored this approach. First, the
number of variables specified in chapter 2 is large relative
to the sample size. Second, as already noted, most continuous variables are not normally distributed. Third, as mentioned above, the data are widely dispersed. Fourth, theory
about the influence of the independent variables on entrant business performance is not so strong that a complete
regression equation could be specified a priori. These four
reasons argued against using regression analysis.

The cross-tabular analysis is conducted by dividing the
sample into three or two groups and comparing the means
and medians of each group. In most analyses, the cut-
points were chosen to occur on natural breaks in the data
rather than to obtain equal sized subsamples.

The explanatory power of the independent variables was
assessed by the R^2, which here, as in regression, is a measure of the fraction of the variance in the dependent variable accounted for by knowing the value of the independent variable.

As noted above, the nature of the data meant that, strictly
speaking, none of the usual statistical testing procedures
were valid. Nevertheless, the differences among means in
the cross-tabulated cells were tested for significance in
order to provide the reader with some indication of confidence about the observed differences. The assumption
that the independent variables might affect the standard
deviation as well as the mean of the dependent variable
seemed the more reasonable and was adopted throughout
this research. This assumption, together with three cell
means, meant that the usual F-test of significance was not
applicable. Instead, the difference between two cell
means at a time was tested and the probability estimated
that the observed sample statistics could have been obtained if the true population values had the opposite sign.
This probability estimate can be interpreted as an ordinary
classical one-tailed significance measure against the null
hypothesis that the true subpopulation means are equal.[2]

---

2. But, to emphasize again, this interpretation is only appropriate if the sample
is random, which, of course, it is not.

Alternatively, it can be thought of as the probability that the difference between the true subpopulation means will have a sign opposite from that shown by the two cell means.

No significance level is applied to these probabilities in the sense of rejecting or not rejecting a hypothesis. The nature of the data and the exploratory nature of the research argued against formal hypothesis testing. Under these circumstances, it seemed quite inappropriate to dismiss a trend in the data because the probability of a reversal of sign, assuming a diffuse prior distribution, was, for example, 0.09 or 0.12 instead of 0.05 or lower (the usual level of confidence). In this study, probabilities below 0.21 have been shown. The approach to analyzing the data was on Bayesian lines—for example, a conclusion could be: "The trend across the three means is in the same direction, the medians display similar behavior, but the probability of a reversed sign on the difference between the low mean and the high mean is 0.16. Therefore, although this trend is indicative considerable caution is required in what one does with the finding." Showing probabilities up to as high as 0.20 enables readers to make their own judgments in a similar manner. This method of presentation involves the reader in the interpretation of the data and a more fruitful reading of this research should be the result. At the same time, I do make clear statements showing my interpretation and judgment of the data throughout the study.

It should be emphasized again: the structural analysis in chapters 7, 8, 9, and 10 is a tentative first step, with highly skewed and dispersed data, in understanding the variation in entrant business performance. The statistics used are applied in the spirit of providing rough guidelines of significance. The conclusions that emerge from this analysis are based on judgments, rather than on formal tests of hypotheses.

Author's Note: Samples of the questionnaires used in collecting data for this study are available by contacting me directly in care of the Division of Research, Harvard Business School, Boston, MA 02163. ERB.

4. Financial Performance

THE FIRST RESEARCH OBJECTIVE of this study is to establish the typical performance of entrant businesses started by established firms. This chapter presents data showing the financial performance of the sample during the first four years of their existence. Data on market performance are presented in chapter 5. These financial data are then compared with another sample of businesses from the PIMS data base for which data exist on their second four years of existence. This combination of two cross-section samples from two projects provides an eight-year history of entrant business unit performance.

FINANCIAL PERFORMANCE: FIRST TWO YEARS

According to this sample of entrant businesses, losses are severe through the first four years of entry (see table 3). Return on investment (ROI) for the median business was −40 percent, mean −78 percent, in the first two years. The standard deviation around the mean was 108 percent, demonstrating a large variability in entrants' performance. The most negative accounting ROI was −442 percent, while the most positive was 80 percent. Only four businesses out of forty achieved a positive net income in their first year of operation. Performance on the pretax profit/sales revenue ratio and cash flow/sales revenue ratio present a similar picture of negative returns, wide dispersion, and skewness.

TABLE 3. FINANCIAL PERFORMANCE OF 40 ENTRANT
BUSINESSES, FIRST TWO YEARS

Percentage *Financial Measures*	*Mean*	*Median*	*(Standard Deviation)*	*Maximum*	*Minimum*
Pretax return on investment[a]	−78	−40	(108)	80	−442
Cash flow/ investment[b]	−103	−83	(58)	−24	−266
Pretax return on sales[c]	−94	−52	(121)	44	−526
Cash flow/sales[d]	−127	−92	(102)	−13	−454
Gross margin/sales[e]	12	20	(34)	80	−67

[a] Net pretax income/average investment. Income is calculated after deduction of corporate expenses but prior to interest charges. Investment is calculated as working capital plus fixed capital (valued at net book value).

[b] Cash generated by aftertax earnings *minus* cash absorbed by increased working capital and increased *net* investment in plant and equipment.

[c] Income defined as in note a as a percentage of sales and lease revenues.

[d] Net income times one-half minus all investment in year 1 and incremental investment in years $t + 1$ as a percentage of sales and lease revenues.

[e] Sales revenues minus purchases, manufacturing, and depreciation as a percentage of sales and lease revenues.

Cash flow/investment, a measure of cash recovery from the new venture, showed a median of −80 percent, mean −103 percent, in the first two years. No entrant business had a positive cash flow in the first two years.

Gross margin/sales at 12 percent is the measure showing the most favorable financial performance. Out of forty entrant businesses, twenty-eight, or 70 percent, reported a positive gross margin/sales ratio. Marketing and R&D expenses are, of course, excluded when calculating gross margin. These findings suggest, therefore, that initially high marketing and R&D expenses were major contributors to the poor financial results. The sample mean marketing/sales revenue was 41 percent, median 35 percent, as shown in table 4. R&D/sales revenue mean ratio was 51 percent, median 26 percent. These ratios demonstrate that entry is particularly demanding on these two expense items in the early years. To put this point another way, mean marketing and R&D costs amounted to 92 percent of the sales dollar, about the same as the 89 percent of the

TABLE 4. OPERATING AND CAPITAL STRUCTURE RATIOS OF 40
ENTRANT BUSINESSES, FIRST TWO YEARS

Percentage Operating Ratios	Mean	Median	(Standard Deviation)	Maximum	Minimum
Pretax return on sales	−94	−52	(122)	44	−526
Purchasing/sales	47	45	(19)	97	9
Manufacturing/sales[a]	39	30	(29)	109	10
Marketing/sales	41	35	(38)	163	0
R&D/sales	51	26	(71)	352	0

Percentage Capital Structure Ratios					
Inventory/sales[a]	37	24	(40)	233	50
Receivables/sales	18	16	(9)	46	6
Net book value/sales[b]	98	51	(149)	783	0
Investment/sales[c]	140	98	(152)	912	40

[a] Service businesses excluded.

[b] One outlier of 2615% excluded (if included mean = 159% and deviation = 424%).

[c] One outlier of 3200% excluded (if included mean = 217% and deviation = 500%).

first two years' sales revenue dollar spent on purchasing inputs and manufacturing the product.

These data suggest that the problem with new businesses is not so much that high capital requirements lower initial returns. Rather, the problem is that there is no return at all—net income is negative—partly because of high marketing and R&D expenses. Furthermore, these expenses do not create a tangible asset, which adds to the riskiness of launching new businesses. Unfortunately, the disguised data do not permit analysis of the absolute dollar magnitudes involved. But we can repeat that the companies contributing these new businesses to the sample were members of the *Fortune* top 200 and each new business was a "significant" venture to its parent company. One imagines therefore that the dollar losses reported by this

sample are not trivial, which further emphasizes the risks
and the difficulties in the early years.

TIME HELPS

On the brighter side, new entrant performance did improve with time. The ratios were about half as negative in
the second two years as they were in the first two, as table
5 shows. For example, mean ROI improved to −43 percent, from −78 percent in the first two years. Obviously,
a key to this improvement lies in lower operating ratios.
Table 6 compares median and mean operating ratios in the
first and second two years of entry. Big reductions occurred
in three operating and one capital ratio: R&D mean expenditures dropped from 51 percent of sales in the first
two years to 23 percent, marketing mean expenditures
dropped from 41 percent to 25 percent, manufacturing/
sales dropped from 39 percent to 28 percent, and invest-
ment/sales dropped from 140 percent to 101 percent.

Improvement in these ratios over the two time periods
could arise from increased volume, lower absolute expenditures, or a combination of both. The data suggest that
the improvement in both operating and capital structure
ratios, with the exception of R&D/sales, came from increased sales revenues. Specifically, median sales revenues grew 49 percent per year through the first four years
of operations (see table 7). In fact, only one business out

TABLE 5. FINANCIAL PERFORMANCE OF 28 ENTRANT
BUSINESSES, SECOND TWO YEARS

Percentage *Financial Measures*[a]	*Mean*	*Median*	*(Standard* *Deviation)*
Pretax return on investment	−43	−14	(98)
Cash flow/investment	−48	−34	(57)
Pretax return on sales	−35	−8	(94)
Cash flow/sales	−50	−27	(100)
Gross margin/sales	26	26	(19)

[a] Definitions of measures shown in table 1.

TABLE 6. COMPARISON OF OPERATING AND CAPITAL
STRUCTURE RATIOS OF 40 ENTRANT BUSINESSES,
FIRST FOUR YEARS

Percentage Operating Ratios	Years 1 and 2 (n = 40)		Years 3 and 4 (n = 28)	
	Mean	*Median*	*Mean*	*Median*
Purchasing/sales	47	45	45	45
Manufacturing/sales[a]	39	30	28	29
Marketing/sales	41	35	25	21
R&D/sales	51	26	23	10
Percentage Capital Structure Ratios				
Inventory/sales[a]	37	24	49	24
Receivables/sales	18	16	18	13
Investment/sales[b]	140	98	101	77

[a] Three service businesses excluded.
[b] One outlier excluded.

of the twenty-eight with four years of data suffered a decline in sales revenue. All outlay items grew as well, but, with the exception of purchases expenditures, they grew at a *lesser* rate than sales revenues. For example, marketing expenditures for the median business grew at 41 percent per year. In numbers of businesses, twenty-five out of the twenty-eight entrants with four years of data—or 90 percent of the sample—had much higher absolute marketing expenses in their fourth year, compared with their first year of operations.

The increase in marketing expenses comes as a surprise. Studies of new product launches show that marketing expenses decline after the first year or so (Buzzell and Nourse 1967). One explanation may be that the results here are for new businesses, not new products. Another might be that, for most of these businesses, sales force expenditures represented almost half their marketing expenses in the first two years and climbed to two-thirds in their second two years. Sales force expenditures, therefore, increased with volume and outweighed reductions in ad-

TABLE 7. ANNUAL PERCENTAGE CHANGE IN ABSOLUTE
OPERATING EXPENDITURES AND SALES REVENUES FOR
ENTRANTS WITH FOUR YEARS OF DATA

	Annual Percentage Change Years 1 through 4 (n = 28)		
	Mean	*(Standard Deviation)*	*Median*
Sales Revenues	87	(86)	49
Operating Items			
Purchasing expenditures	88	(98)	57
Manufacturing expenditures	75	(106)	46
Marketing expenditures	51	(59)	41
R&D expenditures	33	(83)	1
Inputs and Selling Prices			
Index of materials costs	3.8	(5)	3.7
Index of hourly wage rates	7.0	(3.6)	5.9
Index of selling prices	1.3	(7.3)	1.9
Price-cost squeeze[a]	-3.1	(7.4)	-1.5
Capital Structure Items			
Receivables	84	(78)	49
Inventory	65	(67)	45
Investment	61	(63)	37

[a] Selling price growth minus purchases and manufacturing expenditures growth.

vertising expenses. In turn, the preponderance of sales force expenditures for most of the businesses probably reflects the fact that this sample deals primarily in industrial goods. For example, mean sales force/sales revenue ratio for the industrial businesses in the first two years was 22 percent, and for the consumer businesses 6 percent; conversely the advertising and promotion/sales revenue ratio was 7 percent for industrial businesses, 44 percent for consumer businesses.

R&D expenses also did not decline through the first four years, but at 1 percent growth per year they showed, on average, nothing like the growth in marketing expenditures. Even so, sixteen businesses, or about half the four-year sample, had absolute R&D expenses in the fourth year double their level in the first year. Product R&D represented three-quarters of all R&D expenses and process R&D accounted for the remainder. Perhaps this emphasis on product R&D means that repeated adjustments were made to the product during these early years. As with marketing expenses, consumer and industrial entrants varied in their R&D intensity: 59 percent R&D/sales revenue ratio for industrial businesses, 22 percent for consumer.

Purchase expenditures grew at 57 percent per year, almost 10 points more than the growth in sales revenues. This faster growth was partially due to increased input prices, as demonstrated by a 3.7 percent annual increase in the purchase price of materials. Another possible explanation is that repeated product adjustments, if they occurred, made it difficult to manage the purchasing function efficiently.

Manufacturing expenses grew at 46 percent per year, somewhat lower than sales revenues. Slower growth in manufacturing expenses suggests that some learning economies occurred, particularly as the median hourly wage rate increased 5.9 percent per year.

Manufacturing and purchasing expenditures combined rose faster than sales revenues. This fact puts particular emphasis on pricing policy. In fact, according to this sample, while new businesses can count on rising materials and wage costs, they cannot count on matching price increases. Prices rose only 1.9 percent per year, according to table 7. The result was a price-cost squeeze that amounted to an annual increase in manufacturing and purchase costs 1.5 percent greater than the annual increase in prices.

Finally in table 7 we see that the median increase in investment, at 37 percent, was considerably lower than the growth in sales revenues. Lower investment growth means that capacity utilization increased; in the first two years, median capacity utilization was 47 percent, in the second two years, it was 67 percent.

This analysis of the behavior of costs and sales revenues leads to an important management implication: the key to improvement in financial performance is to get rapid sales growth with a less than proportionate rate of increase in outlays on operating and capital items. This seemingly obvious statement is different from the widespread approach of forecasting improvement because of a decline in expenditures. Usually, the largest decline is forecast on marketing and R&D expenses. Very often, forecasts will also show manufacturing and purchases expenditures with either no increase or only a slight increase in costs and wages. According to this sample, both expenses and capital items go only one way—up.

LOSSES FOR HOW LONG?

Severe losses over the first four years of operations raise the question of how long, on average, corporate new ventures take to improve their performance. To answer this question, the data just presented were combined with two samples of businesses in more advanced stages of development extracted from the PIMS data base. One of these samples was a group of businesses with data on their fifth through eighth years of operations; these businesses were called adolescents. The other sample was a group of businesses that, on average, were eighteen years old and described their product or service as "mature"; these businesses can be regarded as established and were named mature. These samples allowed a comparison of performance over three stages of business development: start-up (the entrant business sample), adolescence, and maturity (the two PIMS samples).

It appears that entrant business units need, on average, about eight years before they reach profitability. Note in table 8 that ROI did not become positive until the seventh and eighth years, with the median business earning 7 percent. However, the adolescents still have some way to go before attaining the 17 percent reported by mature businesses. In fact, a simple time projection of the results in the first eight years suggests that ten to twelve years will elapse before the ROI of the entrants equals that of mature businesses. Figures drawn from this comparison must be regarded as estimates because I cannot be sure that the businesses in the adolescent and mature business samples were, in their first four years, structurally similar to the

TABLE 8. COMPARISON OF FINANCIAL PERFORMANCE OF 40 ENTRANT BUSINESSES OVER EIGHT YEARS AND AGAINST ESTABLISHED BUSINESSES

Percentage of Financial Measures		Entrants in Start-up Phase		Adolescent Businesses		Established Businesses
		Years 1 and 2 (n = 40)	*Years 3 and 4 (n = 28)*	*Years 5 and 6 (n = 61)*	*Years 7 and 8 (n = 61)*	*Avg. Age 18 Years (n = 454)*
Pretax return on investment	Mean	−78	−43	−5	5	21
	(Standard deviation)	(108)	(98)	(27)	(19)	(20)
	Median	−39	−14	−8	7	17
Pretax return on sales	Mean	−94	−35	−13	1	10
	(Standard deviation)	(122)	(94)	(33)	(16)	(9)
	Median	−52	−8	−5	−4	9
Cash flow/sales	Mean	−127	−50	−10	−5	2
	(Standard deviation)	(102)	(100)	(15)	(11)	(8)
	Median	−92	−27	−13	−4	3
Gross margin/sales	Mean	12	26	22	24	27
	(Standard deviation)	(34)	(19)	(19)	(17)	(12)
	Median	20	26	19	22	26

businesses in the entrant business sample. However, even if we limit accuracy to ±2 or 3 years, this length of time to reach profitability is not encouraging.

Cash flow does not become positive at all, for the median business, in the first eight years. A similar time projection suggests that twelve years are needed before entrants generate cash flow ratios similar to those of mature businesses.

Entrants approach the gross margin–to–sales ratio of established businesses quickly in comparison with their performance on the other three measures, because, as already pointed out, this measure excludes marketing and R&D expenditures. By their second two years of commercialization, entrants had already attained almost the same level of gross margin/sales (26 percent) as established businesses (27 percent); levels in succeeding years were close to that of established businesses.

It is an understatement to say that these results demonstrate that corporate diversification is difficult. Negative financial performance as large as seen in this sample of entrants, and for as long as eight years or more according to the adolescent and mature samples, is not an appealing investment opportunity for established firms. Indeed, some corporations would not tolerate such performance for so long. And, to make matters worse, it is worth emphasizing that this sample is a sample of survivors. Presumably, therefore, performance of a sample of *all* corporate diversification businesses ever launched would be even worse.

The Probability of Profits

Another way of looking at the hazards of entry is presented in table 9 which shows the number of businesses with positive profits in each year for both the new entrant and adolescent samples. In the new entrant sample, ten businesses out of twenty-eight, or 36 percent, had positive net income in the fourth year. In the adolescent sample, twenty-seven entrants out of sixty-one, or 44 percent, recorded positive results in the third two years. Odds improve in years seven and eight—again, assuming survival for that length of time—with thirty-nine profitable busi-

TABLE 9. FREQUENCY DISTRIBUTION OF PROFITABLE
BUSINESSES BY YEARS OF COMMERCIALIZATION

Years of Commercialization	Sample Size	Positive Net Income (Number of Businesses)	Percentage of Sample with Positive Net Income
1	40	4	10
2	40	7	18
3	36	10	28
4	28	10	36
Adolescent Sample			
5–6	61	27	44
7–8	61	39	64

nesses out of sixty-one, or 64 percent, for a two-in-three chance of being profitable by the fourth two years.

Presumably, managers expect more than just the avoidance of negative profits. A more relevant question might be, "What are the chances of earning a normal return in what time span?" The mean pretax accounting ROI for the established businesses in the PIMS project was 21 percent, a figure that can serve as the value of a normal return. The question can therefore be rephrased to, "How many entrants earn higher than 21 percent ROI in each time period?" The answer is one out of forty in the first two years (3 percent), one out of twenty-eight in the second two years (4 percent), eight out of sixty-one in the third two years (13 percent), and seven out of sixty-one in the fourth two years (11 percent). Effectively, therefore, these figures mean that an entrant has about a one-in-ten chance of earning a normal return in the third two years, assuming it survives that long. These chances of earning a normal return merely underline what has already become clear: entry is financially unrewarding for periods longer than most managers' horizons.

Obviously, improved financial performance over eight years results from improvement in either operating or capital structure ratios, and it is interesting to see which of these did, in fact, improve. Table 10 shows these ratios together with the steady-state values of established businesses. Two of the operating ratios—marketing/sales and

R&D/sales—showed considerable improvement but still took eight years to get close to the mean and median of established businesses. The purchases/sales ratio made little progress over the eight years toward the steady-state value, an outcome for which the price-cost squeeze was at least partially responsible.

Of the capital items, inventory/sales and investment/ sales took eight years to approach those of established businesses, although the latter was still some 19 points short of the 60 percent investment/sales ratio of established businesses.

ADJUSTED RETURN ON INVESTMENT

Both managers and various students of business have queried the conventional accounting treatment of marketing and R&D expenses (Friedman 1973; Bloch 1974; Siegfried and Weiss 1974; Weiss 1969). The argument is that marketing and R&D expenditures are made with the objective of differentiating a business from its rivals over the long term, in this case, to differentiate the entrant from businesses already operating in the entered market. Eventually, managers expect to lower the cross-elasticities of demand among the rival products or services so that they can price above marginal cost or gain a larger market share, or achieve both. Current outlays of marketing and R&D expenditures for future benefit are, therefore, creating an intangible asset that should be capitalized and depreciated over time.

This point is of considerable importance to managers and to the ways in which corporate diversification business units are evaluated internally. For example, many of the businesses in this sample had negative income but positive gross margin. It can be argued that a business should not be terminated when it is losing money if the gross margin is positive because the marketing and R&D expenses, the cause of the income losses, are creating the future of the business. This suggestion leads to the idea that the effects on ROI of capitalizing marketing and R&D expenditures should be explored.

TABLE 10. OPERATING AND CAPITAL STRUCTURE RATIOS OF ENTRANT BUSINESSES IN START-UP AND ADOLESCENT PHASES AND OF ESTABLISHED BUSINESSES

Percentage Operating Ratios	Entrants in Start-up Phase		Adolescent Businesses		Established Businesses
	Years 1 and 2 (n = 40)	*Years 3 and 4 (n = 28)*	*Years 5 and 6 (n = 61)*	*Years 7 and 8 (n = 61)*	*Avg. Age 18 Years (n = 454)*
Purchasing/sales					
Mean	47	45	48	46	39
Median	45	45	47	45	39
Manufacturing/sales[a]					
Mean	39	28	29	26	30
Median	30	29	28	27	29
Marketing/sales					
Mean	41	25	13	12	10
Median	35	21	9	8	8
R&D/sales					
Mean	51	23	6	3	3
Median	26	10	4	3	2.5

Percentage Capital Structure Ratios					
Inventory/sales[a]					
Mean	37	49	25	21	21
Median	24	24	24	17	19
Receivables/sales					
Mean	18	18	22	21	16
Median	16	13	15	14	14
Investment/sales[b]					
Mean	140	101	101	79	60
Median	98	77	84	69	58

[a] Three service businesses excluded.
[b] One outlier excluded.

Before making this exploration, however, three practical problems must be addressed: first, the amount of the outlays that should be capitalized; second, the length of time over which the outlays should be depreciated; and, third, the salvage value of the intangible asset.

It can be argued that not all marketing and R&D outlays should be capitalized because a portion serves to produce current sales and earnings. A counter to this point is that many managers believe that there are intertemporal dependency relations in demand: that is, sales tomorrow are partially a function of sales today. From this point of view, even that portion of outlays designed to obtain sales in the current period is an investment in future sales and earnings. This viewpoint seems particularly applicable to entrant businesses which, apart from their lack of current earnings presented above, have presumably made an entry on the basis of the discounted present value of future earnings. Current expenses, and losses, are tolerated in the hope that the intangible asset created will yield future profits sufficient to recoup them in the long term. For entrant businesses, therefore, persuasive reasons favor capitalizing the entire amount of marketing and R&D expenses.

This conclusion seems more justifiable for R&D expenses: whether they be product or process in nature, practically all their output is likely to extend beyond the current period. On the other hand, marketing expenses, beyond some initial, introductory period, seem to have less durability. Even after recognizing intertemporal demand dependencies, the familiar marketing proposition remains that some marketing outlays need continuation in order that the benefits from earlier expenditures continue to exist. In this sense, at least some marketing expenditures are similar to the maintenance expenses on plant and equipment—which, of course, are expensed. Consequently, a compromise solution was adopted here in which 100 percent of marketing expenses in the first two years of entry and 50 percent in the third and fourth years were capitalized. All R&D expenses in each of the four years were capitalized.

Estimating the length of time over which to capitalize

and depreciate marketing and R&D entails an assessment of the durability of the intangible asset. In a study of the drug industry, Friedman (1973) capitalized 90 percent of R&D expenditures over twenty years, "of which five years is the estimated average elapsed period before commercial introduction and 15 years is estimated average productive term of R&D investment" (p. 26). Friedman also adjusted past R&D outlays for inflation by converting them into current dollars at the rate of 5 percent per year. These adjustments were amortized by the straight-line method. In a study of advertising and corporate taxes in consumer and producer good industries, Weiss (1969) depreciated advertising over six years. He used the double-declining balance method, with a switch to straight-line at the most favorable year.

In assessing durability, we can take advantage of data presented earlier: it takes about eight years for entrant businesses to approach the financial operating character- istics of established businesses and between ten and twelve years to match their financial performance. Ob- viously, it would take several more years to recoup past losses. Furthermore, it is reasonable to assume that new *businesses* have been created by their parent companies with the intention of being long-lived, that is, as perma- nent as the environment will allow. This assumption could not be made about some new *products*. These considera- tions led to the selection of an economic life of twenty years for both marketing and R&D expenses on new en- trant businesses. The double-declining balance method of depreciation is simulated by depreciating at the rate of 10 percent per year. Past outlays are not adjusted for inflation. Finally, on the third problem it was decided to assume zero salvage value.

To distinguish these adjustments from ROI, the result- ing adjusted return is called capitalized ROI. The results of these adjustments to ROI for entrant businesses are shown in table 11. The first column of the table shows that ROI under the accounting definition is −78 percent in the first two years of entry, but, in the second column, ROI under the capitalization definition is 0.1 percent. That is, capitalization and depreciation of marketing and R&D

TABLE 11. COMPARISON OF ACCOUNTING ROI AND ROI
ADJUSTED FOR CAPITALIZATION

Years 1 and 2 (n = 40)	Accounting ROI (percent)	ROI Adjusted for Capitalization (percent)[a]
Mean	−78	0.1
(Standard deviation)	(108)	(23)
Median	−39	0.1
Maximum	80	86
Minimum	−442	−59
Years 3 and 4 (n = 28)		
Mean	−43	3.0
(Standard deviation)	(48)	(19)
Median	−14	6
Maximum	36	55
Minimum	−511	−41

[a] Twenty-year economic life, no salvage value, double-declining balance approximated by depreciating 10% per year; 100% of R&D capitalized, 100% of marketing in first two years and 50% in second two years.

expenditures over a twenty-year economic life, double-declining balance method and assuming no salvage value, moved ROI about seventy-eight points. At the same time, the capitalized ROI measure is more normally distributed: the median is now the same as the mean and the negative left skewness of the accounting ROI measure has been pulled in from a minimum of −442 percent to −59 percent on the capitalized measure. A similar effect occurs in the second two years.

I believe that the capitalized ROI measure provides a better view of the performance of corporate diversification businesses than does accounting ROI. It recognizes the investment characteristic of the two primary causes of large income losses. In capital budgeting systems where ROIs of all the company's businesses are compared as one means of allocating resources, a corporate venture stands a fairer chance of obtaining resources with the capitalized measure than with the accounting measure. Of course, capitalization—even for internal reporting—is a controversial issue and a better solution would be to change the corporate capital budgeting system. But where that is not likely, capitalized ROI provides a partial solution.

ENTRANTS' COST DISADVANTAGE

So far, operating expenditures have been studied in relation to sales revenues and time. An equally important consideration is their relationship to the costs of competitors already operating in the entered market. Managers of the entrant businesses in this sample were asked to estimate the average level of their direct costs—material, production, and distribution items—on a per unit basis, relative to that of leading competitors. The average level for leading competitors was set at 1.0 and managers estimated their percentage cost advantage or disadvantage by adding to or subtracting from 1.0. For example, an entrant business with an estimated direct cost disadvantage relative to incumbents of 10 percent would answer 1.10.

Most of the entrants in this sample were at a cost disadvantage. About 60 percent, or twenty-four out of forty entrants, were at a cost disadvantage in the first two years of entry, 18 percent or seven entrants matched incumbents' costs, and 20 percent or eight had lower direct costs. Of the twenty-eight entrants with four years of data, seventeen or 63 percent began with a cost disadvantage, six matched, and five beat, incumbents' costs. By the second two years, eleven of the eighteen at an initial disadvantage had lessened the magnitude of the disadvantage, but only two had managed to equal or lower their costs below the incumbents. The eleven entrants that initially beat or equaled incumbents' costs continued to do so in their second two years of entry.

The magnitude of entrants' cost disadvantage is shown in table 12. In the first two years of entry, the sample's mean relative cost position was 1.23, but the median at 1.05 indicates that the sample is considerably skewed. In the second two years, entrants lessened their mean relative cost disadvantage to 1.10, or a 10 percent cost handicap, and the median stayed at 1.05. This improvement occurred

TABLE 12. ESTIMATES OF ENTRANTS' COST DISADVANTAGE,
FIRST FOUR YEARS

Relative Direct Costs	Years 1 and 2 ($n = 38$)	Years 3 and 4 ($n = 28$)
Mean[a]	1.23[a]	1.10
(Standard deviation)	(0.47)	(0.29)
Median	1.05	1.05
Maximum	2.75	2.05
Minimum	0.80	0.73

[a] Two outliers of 4.75 and 4.6 excluded.

because entrants with an initial severe relative cost disadvantage were able to improve their position.

Entrants' judgments on their prices and costs, relative to incumbents, were combined into one ratio to see whether they could make up their higher relative costs with higher relative prices. Most businesses could not cover their higher relative costs: specifically, the mean in the first two years was 0.93, indicating a 7 percent relative price/relative cost disadvantage. In the second two years, entrants improved their position on average with a relative price/relative cost ratio of 0.97. In general, therefore, entrants were at a cost disadvantage and could not overcome this with higher relative prices.

5. Market Performance

IF THERE IS LITTLE TO BE ENTHUSIASTIC ABOUT over entrants' financial performance, there is somewhat more basis for satisfaction over their market performance. Nearly all entrants experienced remarkable rates of growth in sales revenues and a few were able to achieve a significant market share. Specifically, table 13 indicates that the mean

TABLE 13. ANNUAL PERCENTAGE CHANGE IN NOMINAL AND REAL SALES REVENUES FOR 28 ENTRANTS WITH FOUR YEARS OF DATA

Sample Statistics	Nominal Annual Change Sales Revenues (Percent) (n = 28)	Real Annual Change Sales Revenues (Percent) (n = 28)
Mean	83	82
(Standard deviation)	(88)	(102)
Median	45	45
Range	−28 to 331	−30 to 402

Frequency Distribution	Entrants with Nominal Change	Entrants with Real Change	
		Number	Percent
Loss in sales revenues	1	1	4
0–20% gain	2	4⎫	
21–40% gain	6	7⎭	39
41–60% gain	6	3⎫	
61–80% gain	2	3⎭	21
81–100% gain	2	4⎫	
More than 100% gain	9	6⎭	36
	28	28	100

annual percentage change in sales revenues for the twenty-eight entrants with four years of data was 83 percent, with a range of −28 to 331 percent. The median annual percentage change was 45 percent. Because the sample's mean selling price growth was only slightly over 1 percent, real sales growth at 82 percent was similar to the nominal growth of 83 percent.

The frequency distribution of individual business average annual percentage changes in nominal and real sales is also shown in table 13. Only one entrant experienced a negative percent change in real sales over the first four years of entry. The remaining twenty-seven entrants were split into three broad groups: eleven (39 percent) experienced a real gain in sales revenues of up to 40 percent per year; six (21 percent) grew at a rate between 41 percent and 80 percent per year; and ten (36 percent) grew in excess of 80 percent per year, with two of these growing at 330 percent per year.

SHARE PERFORMANCE

In spite of these impressive growth rates, entrants' performance on market share and relative market share was not so satisfactory. According to the data in table 14, thirty-seven entrants with complete market share data for themselves and their top three competitors achieved a median share of 7 percent in the first two years of entry. In the second two years the sample median rose by 1 point to 8 percent for the twenty-five entrants with complete share data for themselves and incumbents.

For comparison, table 14 also shows summary share statistics for adolescent and established businesses. The median share of adolescents at 9 percent is one point higher. As one would expect, share performance of entrant businesses was considerably short of the 21 percent median and 23 percent mean share of established businesses. What is disturbing, however, is that the adolescent businesses, after eight years of commercialization, were still so far behind the share performance of the established businesses.

TABLE 14. MARKET SHARE STATISTICS FOR ENTRANTS, ADOLESCENTS, AND ESTABLISHED BUSINESSES AND FREQUENCY DISTRIBUTION FOR ENTRANTS AND ADOLESCENTS

Market Share Percentages	Entrants in Start-up Years 1 and 2 (n = 37)	Years 3 and 4 (n = 25)	Adolescent Businesses Years 5 through 8 (n = 61)	Established Businesses in PIMS (n = 454)
Mean	15	15	15	23
(Standard deviation)	(20)	(19)	(16)	(16)
Median	7	8	9	21

Market Share Frequency Distribution	Entrants (Years 1 and 2) Number	Percent	Entrants (Years 3 and 4) Number	Percent	Entrants (Years 5 through 8) Number	Percent
Less than 1% share	7 }		3 }		0 }	
1–10% share	16 }	62	13 }	64	31 }	51
11–20% share	6 }		4 }		16 }	
21–30% share	1 }	19	0 }	16	2 }	30
More than 30% share	7	19	5	20	12	20
	37	100	25	100	61	100

The frequency distribution of entrants' market share in table 14 shows that they are scattered over a wide range, with a preponderance holding a very low share. In fact, twenty-three entrants out of thirty-seven (62 percent) held less than 10 percent share in their first two years of entry, seven (19 percent) held between 11 and 30 percent and another seven (19 percent) held between 35 and 70 percent. In the second two years, the twenty-five entrants were divided over these three share ranges in similar proportions; that is, 64 percent for less than 10 percent share, 16 percent for 11–30 percent share, and 20 percent for 35–70 percent share. Consequently, there was little movement in the frequency distribution over the first four years. In the second four years, however, there was a tendency for the mass of the frequency distribution to move to higher share levels. For example, the proportion of adolescent businesses holding less than 10 percent share dropped from the 62 percent and 64 percent reported above to 51 percent. At the same time, the proportion of businesses holding 11–30 percent share increased from 19 percent and 16 percent to 30 percent. The proportion holding more than 30 percent share was about the same as for businesses in the first four years.

Share improvement, therefore, for the sample as a whole seems to have occurred but at a very slow rate. This judgment does not suggest, of course, that all individual entrant businesses have made slow progress on improving their market share. Of the twenty-five entrants with four years of complete market share data, nine or 36 percent achieved an annual percentage increase in their share greater than 50 percent, twelve (48 percent) achieved an increase under 50 percent annually, and four (16 percent) lost share (see table 15). The high share gainers were those that had a low share in the first two years of entry and the share losers were those with a high initial share. Share losers held a mean 47 percent in their first two years and 33 percent in their second two years. Entrants with a moderate rate of share change held 5.2 percent in their first two years and 8.1 percent in the second two years. Finally, those with a high rate of share change held an average

TABLE 15. ANNUAL PERCENTAGE CHANGE AND ABSOLUTE CHANGE IN MARKET SHARE FOR 25 ENTRANTS WITH FOUR YEARS OF COMPLETE MARKET DATA

Annual Percentage Change in Market Share	Entrants		Years 1 and 2 Mean Market Share (Percent)	Years 3 and 4 Mean Market Share (Percent)
	Number	Percent		
Negative rate of change	4	16	47	33
1–25% gain	9 ⎫	48	5	8
26–50% gain	3 ⎭			
50–100% gain	5 ⎫	36	1	4
More than 100% gain	4 ⎭			
	25	100		
Absolute Change in Market Share				
Lost share points	4	16	47	33
Gained less than 1 share point	9	36	1.6	2.0
Gained 1–4 share points	5	20	3.7	6.1
Gained 4–7 share points	3	12	4.9	10.6
Gained more than 7 share points	4	16	29	38
	25	100		

share of 1.2 percent in their first two years and 4.3 percent in their second two years.

Perhaps a more interesting measure is the absolute number of share points gained or lost between the first and second two years of entry. Table 15 also shows that of the twenty-one entrants that gained share points, nine (36 percent) gained less than one share point. The remaining twelve were split about equally over gains of one to four share points, four to seven share points, and a gain greater than seven share points. This distribution indicates that this sample of entrants did not gain share in either significant amounts or with great rapidity. One reason for this performance (dealt with more fully in chapter 8), is that these entrants were in rapidly growing markets—an average of 49 percent per year over the first four years. Thus, their mean growth in sales of 83 percent, although almost twice the market rate, was insufficient to achieve significant share when starting from zero share.

Again, the PIMS project provides a comparison for these share gains. Buzzell et al. (1975) reported that "among the 600 businesses in the PIMS sample, only about 20 percent enjoyed market share gains of 2 points or more from 1970 to 1972. Of those that have begun operations since 1965, over 40 percent achieved share increases of 2 points or more—compared with only 17 percent of the businesses established before 1950" (p. 103). In this sample of entrants, 42 percent achieved share increases of two points or more, which is similar to the finding reported above for adolescent businesses (those in operation since 1965).

The performance of entrant businesses on relative market share (entrant's share as a percentage of the top three competitors combined) was somewhat similar to their performance on market share (the correlation coefficient between the two measures is 0.84). Table 16 shows that almost half the sample, 41 percent, achieved less than 11 percent relative share; 24 percent achieved a relative share between 11 and 30 percent; and the remainder, 35 percent, held more than 30 percent relative share. This distribution makes the mean relative share of 44 percent in the first two years a particularly misleading summary statistic. The

TABLE 16. RELATIVE MARKET SHARE STATISTICS FOR ENTRANTS, ADOLESCENTS, AND ESTABLISHED BUSINESSES AND FREQUENCY DISTRIBUTION FOR ENTRANTS AND ADOLESCENTS

Relative Share[a] Percentages	Entrants		Adolescent Businesses Years 5 through 8 (n = 61)	Established Businesses in PIMS (n = 454)
	Years 1 and 2 (n = 37)	Years 3 and 4 (n = 25)		
Mean	44	47	36	59
(Standard deviation)	(61)	(79)	(49)	(60)
Median	14	13	18	47

Relative Share[a] Frequency Distribution	Entrants Years 1 and 2		Entrants Years 3 and 4		Adolescents	
	Number	Percent	Number	Percent	Number	Percent
Less than 1% relative share	3 ⎱		1 ⎱		0 ⎱	
1–10% relative share	12 ⎰	41	9 ⎰	40	17 ⎰	28
11–20% relative share	6 ⎱		7 ⎱		12 ⎱	
21–30% relative share	3 ⎰	24	1 ⎰	32	11 ⎰	38
31–60% relative share	3 ⎱		1 ⎱		11 ⎱	
More than 61% relative share	10 ⎰	35	6 ⎰	28	10 ⎰	34
	37	100	25	100	61	100

[a] Defined as respondent's market share divided by sum of shares of top three competitors multiplied by 100.

median of 14 percent seems a fairer reflection of the performance of this sample on relative share.

In the second two years, the mean relative share increased from 44 percent to 47 percent. Most of the sample showed some slight improvement in relative share and three entrants showed a large improvement by moving to relative share positions of 175 percent, 239 percent and 318 percent (in one of these markets, the leading competitor quit, and in the other two, the three leading competitors reduced their output—see incumbent reaction in chapter 10). It seems that significant improvement for most entrants in their relative share does not occur until the second four years. The adolescent businesses in table 16 showed an upward movement in the frequency distribution compared with entrants: businesses with less than 10 percent relative share declined to 28 percent of the sample and those with 11–30 percent rose to 38 percent of the sample. Their median performance was also higher, at 18 percent. However, adolescent businesses are still twenty-nine relative share points short of the 47 percent achieved by established businesses.

6. Linking Financial and Market Performance

NOW THAT THE FINANCIAL AND MARKET PERFORMANCES of this sample of entrants are known, it is appropriate to attempt first some descriptive explanation of the former with the latter. There are persuasive theoretical reasons and a good deal of evidence suggesting a positive association between financial performance and market share. For example, economic theory suggests that production economies of scale are realized as the scale of the operation becomes larger; the higher the market share, the more likely it is that the business is at least of minimum efficient scale. The experience curve theory extends this relationship to accumulated volume and to all costs. There is strong empirical evidence showing that higher relative accumulated volume has lowered all costs on some products (Boston Consulting Group 1970). The PIMS program has shown that businesses with large market shares had much higher ROIs than those with relatively low market shares (Buzzell, Gale, and Sultan 1975).

On the other hand, building share should damage financial performance in the short run. The consequences of a share-building strategy, such as higher marketing expenses, higher quality, lower prices, and capacity extensions, affect adversely both income statements and balance sheets. Buzzell, Gale, and Sultan (1975) and Fruhan (1972) have demonstrated this relationship empirically.

In the same time period, therefore, a positive relationship between financial performance and share would be expected for entrant businesses. Conversely, a negative relationship between financial performance and the rate of change in share should be expected. These two relationships are studied in this chapter.

According to this study's data, the financial performance is less negative, the higher the share. Specifically, table 17 shows that entrants with an average share below 2.2 percent reported ROI of −99 percent, those with share in the range 3.2–11.0 percent recorded an ROI of −58 percent, and those with share above 12 percent had an ROI of −20 percent. That is, ROI was some seventy-nine points less negative between low-share entrants and high-share entrants. There is only a 0.023 probability that the difference could be positive—that is, that mean ROI at the high-share level could be worse than the mean ROI at the low-share level. The medians at −67 percent, −40 percent, and −20 percent respectively illustrate the same trend of improvement.

Table 17 also shows the relationship between two other financial measures and market share. Mean cash flow/investment improved from −119 percent for low-share entrants to −87 percent for medium-share entrants and to −75 percent for high-share entrants. This variable is more normally distributed than ROI and, therefore, the indicated 3 percent probability that the cash flow/investment ratio of high-share entrants could be better than low-share entrants provides some confidence in the observed direction. The medians also show a similar trend. A similar trend is apparent for both median and mean return on sales (pretax profit–to–sales revenue ratio).

The positive relationship between financial performance and higher relative market share is even more pronounced than the relationship with share. One indication of this is that the R^2 results with relative market share in table 17 are double those with share alone. For example, the R^2 on ROI and relative share is 0.29, compared with 0.15 for share alone. Similarly, the R^2 on cash flow/investment is 0.30 for relative share and 0.15 for share. For return on sales, R^2 is 0.25 for relative share and 0.09 for share alone.

Another indication is that median and mean performance was considerably more negative at low levels of *relative* market share than it was at low share. For example,
low relative share businesses recorded a mean ROI of
−118 percent and a median of −93 percent, compared
with −99 percent, median −67 percent, for low-share businesses. At the same time, performance at high relative
share levels was at least as good as seen above on share
and occasionally even better. The net result is even wider
differences between the financial performance of low relative share and high relative share businesses. Thus, high
relative share in the first two years of entry yielded an ROI
of −20 percent; an improvement of ninety-eight points
over low relative share; a cash flow/investment of −71
percent, an improvement of fifty points; and a return on
sales of −30 percent, an improvement of eighty-nine
points.

The positive relationship between financial performance and market share continued to hold in the second
two years of entry. Table 18 shows a big difference between low relative share and high relative share: for example, median ROI for low relative share businesses was
−17 percent, whereas for high-share business it was −3
percent; mean ROI for low-share businesses was −33 percent, for high-share businesses, −7 percent.

WHY DOES SHARE HELP FINANCIAL PERFORMANCE?

In chapter 4, it was seen that entrants, on average, were
at a serious cost disadvantage relative to incumbents. Economic theory suggests that the severity of entrants' relative
cost disadvantage varies inversely with their share. Table
19 shows evidence supporting this prediction, at least for
this sample of entrants.

In the first two years of entry, entrants with a low market
share were at a 29 percent cost disadvantage, whereas
those with a high share suffered a 4 percent disadvantage.
In the second two years, the favorable relationship of share
to entrants' relative costs was more marked. Those with a

TABLE 17. RELATIONSHIP BETWEEN ENTRANTS' FINANCIAL PERFORMANCE AND MARKET SHARE, FIRST TWO YEARS

	Market Share								
	Low 0.1 to 2.2%[a] (n = 12)			Medium 3.2 to 11.0% (n = 12)			High 12.0 to 70.0% (n = 13)		
Financial Measures	Mean	Median	(Standard Deviation)	Mean	Median	(Standard Deviation)	Mean	Median	(Standard Deviation)
Return on investment (R^2 = 0.15, probability = 0.023)[b]	−99	−67	(115)	−58	−40	(69)	−20	−20	(43)
Cash flow/investment (R^2 = 0.15, probability = 0.03)	−119	−95	(67)	−87	−77	(36)	−75	−71	(30)
Return on sales (R^2 = 0.09, probability = 0.068)	−94	−79	(104)	−82	−44	(90)	−36	−36	(52)

| | Relative Market Share | | | | | | | | |
| | Low 0.1 to 3.6% (n = 13) | | | Medium 3.7 to 42.0% (n = 12) | | | High 43.0 to 228% (n = 12) | | |
Financial Measures	Mean	Median	(Standard Deviation)	Mean	Median	(Standard Deviation)	Mean	Median	(Standard Deviation)
Return on investment (R^2 = 0.29, probability = 0.005)	-118	-93	(113)	-28	-40	(48)	-20	-21	(22)
Cash flow/investment (R^2 = 0.30, probability = 0.004)	-129	-110	(64)	-76	-67	(31)	-71	-74	(15)
Return on sales (R^2 = 0.25, probability = 0.012)	-119	-95	(112)	-47	-35	(63)	-30	-21	(39)

[a] Cut-points chosen to obtain equal sized subpopulations as nearly as possible. Gaps between upper and lower extremities of two neighboring subpopulations indicate that no entrant held share between the extremities. The findings were tested for sensitivity to changes in the cut-points.

[b] Probability refers to the probability that the difference in financial performance means between the Low-share subpopulation and the High-share subpopulation will not have the indicated sign. For example, the difference between return on investment at low share is -99%, and at high share, -20%, which comes to a difference of -79%. The test is, "What is the probability that the difference between low and high share could be positive?" In this example, the answer is 0.023, indicating that the two means are not only different but that financial performance at low share is worse than at high share (see chapter 3). Probabilities below .10 suggest that confidence in the result is justified.

TABLE 18. RELATIONSHIP BETWEEN ENTRANTS' FINANCIAL PERFORMANCE AND RELATIVE MARKET SHARE, SECOND TWO YEARS

	Relative Market Share								
	Low 0.1 to 4.5% (n = 8)			*Medium* 7.3 to 16.0% (n = 9)			*High* 24.4 to 318% (n = 8)		
Financial Measures	Mean	Median	*(Standard Deviation)*	Mean	Median	*(Standard Deviation)*	Mean	Median	*(Standard Deviation)*
Return on investment (R^2 = 0.87, probability = 0.09)	−33	−17	(45)	−28	−2	(49)	−7	−3	(17)
Cash flow/investment (R^2 = 0.77, probability = 0.04)	−46	−34	(36)	−34	−22	(37)	−23	−22	(10)
Return on sales (R^2 = 0.63, probability = 0.20)	−17	−13	(30)	−14	−1	(21)	−4	−2	(22)

TABLE 19. RELATIONSHIP BETWEEN ENTRANTS' MARKET
SHARE AND RELATIVE COSTS, FIRST FOUR YEARS

	Market Share		
Years 1 and 2 (n = 37)	Low 4% or Less[a] (n = 16)	Medium 6 to 21% (n = 14)	High 35% or More (n = 7)
Relative direct costs			
Mean	1.29	1.30	1.04
Standard deviation (probability = 0.04)	(0.50)	(0.58)	(0.08)
Years 3 and 4 (n = 25)	(n = 8)	(n = 9)	(n = 8)
Relative direct costs			
Mean	1.31	1.08	0.97
Standard deviation (probability = 0.04)	(0.45)	(0.07)	(0.16)

[a] These cut-points were chosen on the basis of natural breaks in the data rather than on the basis of trying to obtain equal sized subpopulations. As before, the findings were tested for sensitivity to changes in cut-points.

low share reported an average relative cost disadvantage of 31 percent, in contrast to those with high share reporting a 3 percent cost advantage.

Turning to individual cost items, Buzzell, Gale and Sultan (1975) found that the benefits of higher share showed themselves in four major ways. First, rising share had little impact on investment turnover but profit on sales increased sharply. Second, higher share businesses had a lower purchases-to-sales ratio than smaller share businesses. Third, the marketing-to-sales ratio declined as share increased. Fourth, higher share companies seemed able to obtain higher relative prices; they also offered significantly better quality than small-share businesses.

These benefits were observed for entrants in the first two years of entry, as shown in table 20. (This was also true for the second two years, but, for compactness, only the first two years' data are shown.) For example, the investment/sales ratio declined from a mean of 146 percent for low-share entrants to 93 percent for high-share entrants; the medians were 112 percent and 95 percent respectively. Although this difference is not as strong as one

TABLE 20. RELATIONSHIP BETWEEN ENTRANTS' MARKET SHARE, SELECTED RATIOS, AND RELATIVE STRATEGY JUDGMENTS, FIRST TWO YEARS

Ratios	*Low* 4% or Less (n = 16)			*Medium* 6 to 21% (n = 14)			*High* 35% or More (n = 7)		
	Mean	*Median*	*(Standard Deviation)*	*Mean*	*Median*	*(Standard Deviation)*	*Mean*	*Median*	*(Standard Deviation)*
Purchasing/sales (probability = 0.02)	51	53	(17)	45	44	(22)	34	33	(14)
R&D/sales (probability = 0.08)	63	46	(71)	26	17	(31)	25	4	(43)
Marketing/sales (probability = 0.01)	47	41	(43)	37	37	(32)	14	18	(12)
Investment/sales (probability = 0.07)	146[a]	112	(115)	103	101	(62)	93[a]	95	(29)
Strategy Judgments									
Relative product quality (probability = 0.01)	16	9	(62)	48	55	(38)	71	65	(25)
Relative price/relative cost ratio (probability = 0.04)	0.88	0.88	(0.24)	0.95	1.00	(0.22)	1.00	1.00	(0.06)

[a] Outliers of 3,200% and 912% excluded.

would like, the Buzzell, Gale, and Sultan findings on established businesses about the relationship between investment turnover and share increase confidence in this relationship reported for entrant businesses. As regards the improvement in profit/sales, it was apparent from data in table 18 that this does indeed occur as share rises.

Table 20 also shows the applicability of Buzzell's second and third benefits of higher share. The purchases/sales ratio declined from 51 percent at low share to 34 percent at high share. There is only a 2 percent chance that this finding could be reversed. The medians at 53 percent and 33 percent exhibit a similar pattern. Buzzell and associates pointed out that purchases/sales declined as vertical integration, measured by the ratio of value added/sales, increased. This relationship might also apply to entrants; however, because there was a 30 percent chance that the finding could be reversed, these data are not presented. The marketing/sales ratio declined from 47 percent in the first two years to 14 percent in the second two years. The R&D/sales ratio also declined as share rose—from an average of 63 percent at low share to 25 percent at high share.

Finally, entrants with higher share also offer higher quality and are in a better relative price/relative cost position. The average product quality offered by low-share entrants was 16 percent, whereas that offered by those with high shares was 71 percent. There is only a 1 percent chance that this finding could be reversed. In general, the R^2 results between these ratios or judgments and market share were in single figures with the exception of product quality where differing share explained 18 percent of the variability.

Analysis of relative price alone provides ambiguous results, doubtless because of the variability in the entrant sample. Therefore, the relationship between relative price/relative cost and share is analyzed instead. Again, there was a steady improvement in entrants' price/cost position as share rose. Entrants with a low share judged their average relative price/relative cost ratio at 0.88—a disadvantage of 12 percent compared with incumbents. At medium share, the disadvantage was reduced to 5 percent with a ratio of 0.95 and, at high share, entrants estimated that they had achieved price/cost parity with incumbents.

BUILDING SHARE AND FINANCIAL PERFORMANCE

The second relationship under study in this chapter is that between financial performance and the rate of change in share. In the introduction, it was argued that this relationship would be negative in the same time period because of higher costs from a share-building strategy. And indeed, table 21 shows a marked worsening in average financial performance over the first four years of entry as the annual percentage change in relative share increased. Relative share is focused on here because the objective of a "building share" strategy is to improve the relative competitive position of a business, rather than its absolute share position.

Specifically, ROI for the first four years improved from an average of −45 percent, median −20 percent, for rapid share builders to −10 percent, median −4 percent, for those holding share. That is to say, a strategy of rapid relative share building carried a short-term penalty of thirty-five percentage points in mean ROI over the alternative of holding share. As might be expected, rapid share builders also had a worse cash flow/investment ratio than share holders.

The remarkable finding in table 21 is the level of R^2. For example, rate of relative share change explains 88 percent of the variability in ROI and cash flow/investment. Considering the univariate nature of this analysis, an R^2 this high amounts to a quite extraordinary level of explanation of the sample's variability on these measures.

Return on sales (ROS) is also sensitive to relative share change strategy, at least judging by the R^2 of 0.63. However, there is a 17 percent chance that ROS for rapid relative share builders could be higher than that for those holding share. Some caution is, therefore, necessary in interpreting the improvement in mean ROS from −30 percent at the 70 percent or more rate of relative share change

TABLE 21. AVERAGE FINANCIAL PERFORMANCE BY ANNUAL PERCENTAGE CHANGE IN RELATIVE MARKET SHARE, FIRST FOUR YEARS

	Annual Percentage Change in Relative Share								
Four-Year Average Percentage Financial Performance Measure	*Rapid Share Builders 70% or More Increase (n = 8)*			*Moderate Share Builders 12 to 56% Increase (n = 8)*			*Hold Share Less Than 6% Increase (n = 9)*		
	Mean	*Median*	*(Standard Deviation)*	*Mean*	*Median*	*(Standard Deviation)*	*Mean*	*Median*	*(Standard Deviation)*
Return on investment (R^2 = 0.88, probability = 0.06)[a]	−45	−20	(60)	−15	−10	(24)	−10	−4	(18)
Cash flow/investment (R^2 = 0.88, probability = 0.01)	−65	−58	(34)	−20	−20	(9)	−18	−19	(14)
Return on sales (R^2 = 0.63, probability = 0.17)	−18	−24	(32)	−4	−6	(18)	−11	−2	(21)

[a] R^2 measures the fraction of the variance in return on investment accounted for by knowing the rate of share building. Probability, as explained in table 17, refers to the probability that the difference in the financial performance means between the rapid share builders and those holding share will not have the indicated sign.

to the −14 percent average ROS for a holding rate of relative share change.

The impact of changing relative share on the three measures of financial performance is not symmetrical: the big improvement occurred between rapid building and moderate building. For example, mean ROI moved −45 percent, −15 percent, and −10 percent as the rate of relative share change slowed down. Cash flow/investment and return on sales behaved similarly. The reason for this difference appears to be that while both rapid and moderate share builders had higher operating ratios than share holders, moderate builders were able to get a better relative price=cost margin than rapid builders. That is, it seems as if to build share rapidly, an entrant not only has to spend heavily but also be more aggressive on pricing.

The most notable impact of a share-building strategy was on R&D/sales, as shown in table 22. Rapid share builders had a median R&D/sales ratio of 20 percent and moderate share builders reported 17 percent, but share holders reported 3 percent. Share builders also appear to have had higher marketing/sales revenue ratios than share holders. Rapid share builders reported median R&D/sales of 29 percent, about the same as moderate share builders at 28 percent. But share holders reported 17 percent. According to the R^2 measure, about 14 percent of the variability in entrants' marketing/sales ratio was associated with their annual percentage change in relative share.

Investment/sales also showed a tendency to be higher for those entrants changing share rapidly, but there is a good deal of variability in both working and fixed capital ratios and it was not possible to detect an unambiguous relationship between these ratios and rate of share change.

The relative price/relative cost ratios in table 22 indicate that the two subpopulations of share builders differed significantly in their ability to cover their relative costs. Rapid share builders reported a relative price/relative cost ratio of 0.83, median 0.90. Moderate share builders reported 1.02, median 1.00. Moderate share builders, therefore, spent as much, sometimes more, as rapid share builders on increasing their relative share, but managed at the same

TABLE 22. AVERAGE OPERATING RATIOS, CAPITAL RATIOS, AND RELATIVE PRICE/COST RATIOS BY ANNUAL PERCENTAGE CHANGE IN RELATIVE MARKET SHARE, FIRST FOUR YEARS

Four Years Average Ratios	Annual Percentage Change in Relative Share								
	Relative Share Builders						Holders or Relative Share Losers		
	70% or More Increase (n = 8)			12 to 56% Increase (n = 8)			Less Than 6% Increase (n = 9)		
	Mean	Median	(Standard Deviation)	Mean	Median	(Standard Deviation)	Mean	Median	(Standard Deviation)
Marketing/sales ($R^2 = 0.14$)[a]	24	29	(15)	36	28	(32)	23	17	(18)
R&D/sales ($R^2 = 0.29$, probability = 0.05)	19	20	(14)	36	17	(58)	7	3	(9)
Investment/sales ($R^2 = 0.11$)	112	77	(98)	80	88	(31)	86	86	(26)
Relative price/cost ($R^2 = 0.17$, probability = 0.05)	0.83	0.90	(0.17)	1.02	1.0	(0.25)	0.97	0.95	(0.09)

[a] Absence of probability indicates that it was above .20, suggesting little confidence in the mean differences.

time not only to cover these costs but to report a 2 percent price-cost margin advantage over incumbents.

FINANCIAL-MARKET PERFORMANCE CONFLICT

The foregoing analysis of the relationship between financial and market performance points to the conclusion that, within the same time period, the one conflicts with the other. Financial performance worsens, on average, as entrants attempt to improve market performance.

The implications of this conflict for the management of entrant businesses are far-reaching. As newcomers to the market, they must build share to at least a minimum efficient scale. The experience curve proposition would have entrants go one stage further: build share so rapidly that they can surpass the *accumulated* volume of incumbents. But it has been observed that share increases, in terms of absolute points, are small—most entrants achieved 1 percent to 3 percent over the first four years of entry. Given the importance of share in the established phase of a business, it is possible that this sample of entrants did not attempt to build share sufficiently. And yet, if they had, their average financial performance could have been expected to be even worse than reported in chapter 4.

Given the fairly short time horizon of most managers and directors, it seems likely that financial performance is emphasized prematurely. That is, when decisions are being made about price, product quality, sales promotion, and after-sales service, the choice that least impacts short-term financial performance receives preference—particularly in a business that is already showing significant losses and is already two, three, or four years old. While it does reduce the losses, this approach will fail to build market share, thus assuring unsatisfactory financial performance in the long run.

Entrant businesses, on average, cannot, as the old saying goes, have their cake and eat it. If their objective is high share in their served market—and given previous research their objective should seldom be otherwise—they must forgo short-run profits and expect their cash-flow break-even to be a distant event, probably as long as eight years. If entrants, and their parent companies, are not prepared to suffer losses and negative cash flow for that length of time with the objective of gaining a high market share, it would be best for them not to have entered in the first place.

At the same time, it is clear that some entrants were able to achieve significant share quickly, as indicated in chapter 5. It is probable that their ability to do this was connected with the timing of entry and a rapid market growth rate.

It could be argued that the explanation of entrant business financial performance has been completed in this chapter—judging by the high R^2 between financial measures and relative share. However, the key point is that whereas share is a factor explaining satisfactory ROI for established businesses, it is an *objective* for entrant businesses. The analytical framework that follows, therefore, is applied to attempt understanding of both market and financial performance.

7. The Impact of Relatedness on Performance

SIX TYPES OF RELATEDNESS between an entrant business and its parent company were identified in the conceptual scheme presented in chapter 2: technology, scale economy, forward integration, backward integration, marketing, and conglomerate. The first task in this chapter is to formulate operational definitions of these different types and to identify those found in the sample. The second task is to analyze the impact on performance of each type of relatedness. Succeeding chapters deal with the performance impact of market characteristics, entry strategy, and competitive reaction.

MEASURING RELATEDNESS

The operational definitions of relatedness in this study were based on the principle of seeking an objective manifestation of relatedness rather than asking executives' opinions. For example, instead of asking executives if their business was based on, say, a vertical relationship to the parent company, the data forms asked about a manifestation of vertical integration. A forward integration relationship manifests itself by a high percentage of inputs purchased from the parent company. Accordingly, entrant managers were asked to estimate "the percentage of materials and supplies purchased from other components of the same company during the first 2 years." Similarly, a backward integration relationship was captured by asking for an estimate of "the percentage of sales made to other components of the same company." Of course, we must recognize that managers' estimates are subjective. But, by asking them about a particular aspect of each relationship, that is, the way in which each typically manifests itself, one can obtain more objective data.

This procedure was followed for measuring marketing, scale economy, and technology relatedness. Marketing relatedness, which refers primarily to customer knowledge, manifests itself when a high percentage of an entrant's initial sales come from existing channel customers or end customers of the parent company. Consequently, entrant managers were asked to estimate "the percentage of sales which came from previous immediate and end customers of the parent company (during the first 2 years)."

Marketing relatedness could also reveal itself by the entrant's benefiting from existing parent company programs and famous brand names. These manifestations were considered less important than that of high sales to existing customers, but the data were collected to provide as full a picture of entrant-parent company marketing relatedness as possible. The sharing of existing programs was captured by asking entrant managers to estimate the percentage of marketing expenditures spent with the parent company. Usage of company brands was identified by asking for a judgment on whether the entrant business "benefitted from well-known brand names, trade marks or other aspects of goodwill."

Scale economy relatedness manifests itself through the utilization of existing parent company facilities. Consequently, entrant managers were requested to estimate "the percentage of operating plant, equipment and personnel shared with other components of the parent company."

Technology relatedness manifests itself by the existence of a technical knowledge relationship between the entrant and the parent company. Entrant managers were asked whether their business benefited from the parent's trade secrets or proprietary knowledge pertaining to the products or service and pertaining to processes.

These questions total to nine; seven were considered the major questions for classifying the type of relatedness for each entrant business and two—shared marketing programs and famous brand names—were considered minor questions to be used in cases of doubt.

IDENTIFYING RELATEDNESS

The next step was to lay out the rules by which entrant businesses would be assigned to a type of relatedness. Discussion with participating executives suggested that to be assigned to the marketing type of relatedness, an entrant should have obtained more than 75 percent of its sales in the first two years from previous customers of the parent company. To be assigned to the scale economy type, an entrant should have used 80 percent[1] of parent company operating facilities. To be assigned to the technology type of relatedness, an entrant should have benefited from either product or process knowledge. The assignment rule for the vertical integration type was derived from the data.

Distributions of responses to the nine questions appear in table 23. The distribution on the forward integration question shows a natural data break between 10 percent and 20 percent; twenty-eight entrants, or 68 percent of the sample, obtained less than 10 percent of their purchases within the parent company, whereas thirteen, or 32 percent, obtained between 20 percent and 80 percent. Because of this, 20 percent appeared to be a reasonable level where forward integration relatedness might be influential on entrant management. This cut-point means that there

---

1. The difference between 75 percent and 80 percent is not inherently significant. The marketing questions called for an answer in one of four categories: less than 25 percent, 25–49 percent, 50–74 percent, and 75 percent or more. The scale economy question had three categories: less than 10 percent, 10–80 percent, more than 80 percent.

were at least thirteen entrants that met the definition of forward integration relatedness.

The distribution on the backward integration question shows that only five businesses made more than 10 percent of their sales in the first two years to other components of the parent company. Individual inspection[2] of these five businesses revealed that their characteristics were highly dissimilar: they were not, in themselves, a homogeneous group. Accordingly, the backward integration type of relatedness was deleted from this study.

Eight businesses reported that they shared more than 80 percent of their plant, equipment, and personnel with other components of the parent company. Inspection of these businesses indicated that they were not a homogeneous group. Five were clearly forward integration businesses (purchases internally were between 50 and 80 percent) and three were marketing businesses (more than 75 percent of sales from existing customers). Consequently, the scale economy type of relatedness was also dropped from this study. Parenthetically, it should be noted that this outcome could signal either that the wrong question was asked to capture scale economy or that scale economy is a derivative of other types.

The sample distribution on the major marketing questions shows that fourteen entrants reported more than 75 percent of sales in their first two years coming from previous end customers of the parent company. Initially, therefore, these fourteen were assigned to the marketing type of relatedness.

Sixteen entrants reported benefits from either product knowledge or process knowledge. Nine of these benefited from both types of knowledge, five from product knowledge alone, and seven from process knowledge alone. Initially, therefore, sixteen businesses qualified for technology relatedness.

---

2. The inspection procedure utilized program SORLIS which sorts and lists in ascending order the values of one variable against the values of other variables specified by the user. This procedure enables the researcher to personally identify patterns and relationships among the variables—an advantage with a small data base such as this one.

TABLE 23. DISTRIBUTION OF SAMPLE ON PARENT COMPANY RELATEDNESS ITEMS

	Forward Integration (Percentage Purchases Obtained within Parent Company)	Backward Integration (Percentage Sales to Components of Parent Company)	Scale Economy (Percentage Operating Plant Equipment and Personnel Shared within Company)	
0	21	24	10	23
1–10%	7	11	10–80	9
11–20%	0	3	80	8
21–40%	5	2		40
41–60%	2	0		
61%+	6	0		
	40	40		

Marketing Major Questions

	(Percentage Sales to Parent's Previous Immediate Customers)	(Percentage Sales to Previous End Customers)
Less than 25%	17	18
25–49%	4	4
50–74%	7	4
75% or more	12	14
	40	40

Marketing Minor Questions

	(Percentage Marketing Expenditures Spent with Parent Company Marketing Effort)		(Significant Benefit from Parent Brand Names)
	10	18	No = 20
	10–80	12	Yes = 20
	80	10	40
		40	

Technology

(Significant Benefit from Parent Company Product Knowledge?)	(Significant Benefit from Parent Company Process Knowledge?)
No = 26	No = 24
Yes = 14	Yes = 16
40	40

The foregoing procedure left at least three types of relatedness in this sample: forward integration, marketing, and technology. The next step was to examine whether these three types were distinct from each other. This step was performed by studying the correlation matrix of the nine questions and by manual inspection of the whole sample.[3]

The pair-wise correlations in table 24 are, in general, low,[4] and this was taken as a sign of little overlap among the three types. For example, the correlations between the two major marketing questions and the forward integration questions are -0.09 and -0.0 respectively. None of the correlations between pairs of questions for the three types of relatedness are above 0.3.

Next, the individual businesses were examined to see if the businesses met more than one rule for assignment to a type of relatedness. The low correlations created the expectation that most would not, and this proved to be the case. Eight of the entrants with more than 75 percent of sales from previous customers of the parent company did not also meet the forward integration and technology rules. Four entrants with more than 20 percent of internal purchases did not also meet the marketing and technology rules. Eight entrants benefiting from product or process knowledge did not also meet forward integration and marketing rules. These numbers total twenty, meaning that half the sample could be unambiguously assigned to a type of relatedness.

Seven entrants clearly qualified for more than one type of relatedness. Two met all three assignment rules, two

---

3. Again, using program SORLIS.
4. This matrix involves both continuous and discrete variables. Under this circumstance, the interpretability of correlation coefficients and tests of significance against the null hypothesis of no association is not clear. As a guideline, however, it can be noted that, with 38 degrees of freedom, a coefficient of 0.39 or higher is statistically different from zero at a level of 0.01 and 0.31 is statistically significant at a level of 0.05. Another guideline is to argue in terms of dependence and independence. In this case, when y and x are correlated, the amount of reduction in scatter around y achieved by knowing x is calculated by the formula $100 (1 - r^2)$, where $r =$ correlation. Thus, r of, say, 0.3 amounts to a reduction of 5 percent in the scatter around y when correlated with x, in contrast to the scatter around y by itself (Ehrenberg 1975: 237).

TABLE 24. CORRELATION MATRIX OF QUESTIONS REPRESENTING FIVE TYPES OF RELATEDNESS ($n = 40$)

	Forward Integration	Backward Integration		Marketing			Scale Economy	Technology	
	1	2	3	4	5	6	7	8	9
Forward Integration 1	1.00								
Backward Integration 2	0.08	1.00							
3	-0.09	0.22	1.00						
Marketing 4	-0.00	0.12	0.57	1.00					
5	0.27	0.29	0.23	0.17	1.00				
6	-0.01	0.37	0.15	0.22	0.40	1.00			
Scale Economy 7	0.29	0.09	0.20	0.08	0.29	-0.21	1.00		
Technology 8	0.08	0.34	-0.09	-0.16	0.23	-0.05	-0.01	1.00	
9	0.06	0.04	-0.10	-0.25	0.31	0.00	0.01	0.42	1.00

Questions referring to each type of relatedness:

1 = % purchases obtained within parent company?
2 = % sold within parent company?
3 = % sales from previous immediate customers of parent?
4 = % sales from previous end customers of parent?
5 = % marketing expenditures spent with parent company?
6 = benefit or not from parent company brand names?
7 = % operating plant, equipment, personnel shared with parent?
8 = benefit or not from parent company product knowledge?
9 = benefit or not from parent company process knowledge?

were both marketing and technology types, two combined marketing and forward integration relatedness, and one combined technology and forward integration relatedness.

Four entrants met none of the rules for assignment to one of the three types of relatedness. These businesses were assigned to the conglomerate type of relatedness.

These procedures accounted for thirty-one of the businesses, leaving nine still to be assigned. Two of these nine obtained more than 75 percent of their sales from previous customers and reported benefits from process knowledge. However, both also reported benefits from parent company brand names and marketing programs. Because of these characteristics, both businesses were assigned to the marketing type of relatedness. A similar decision was made for a third business that met the marketing assignment rule and reported benefits from product knowledge. A fourth business exhibiting both marketing and technology characteristics reported that although 75 percent of its wholesaler sales came from previous parent company customers, a very low percentage came from previous end users of the parent company. This characteristic caused the business to be assigned to the technology group.

The remaining five entrants included two with 50–75 percent of sales from previous customers and which did not meet other rules. These two were assigned to the marketing group. Two businesses reported benefits from process knowledge but also reported 40 percent and 80 percent of purchases from within the parent company. These high levels of internal purchases resulted in these two being assigned to the forward integration group. The last business reported high internal purchases and benefits from product knowledge; it was also assigned to the forward integration type of relatedness.[5] The assignment rules are summarized in table 25. The breakdown of this sample of entrant businesses on the different types of relatedness was as follows:

---

5. Follow-up questioning of entrant business managers further clarified the appropriate type of relatedness for some of these businesses. This method was not relied on extensively, however, because the methodology goal was to obtain as objective a classification scheme as possible.

	Number	*Percent*
Marketing Relatedness	12	30
Technology	10	25
Forward Integration	7	18
Conglomerate	4	10
All Three Types of Relatedness	2	5
Marketing and Technology	2	5
Marketing and Forward Integration	2	5
Technology and Forward Integration	1	2
	40	100

TABLE 25. RULES FOR ASSIGNING ENTRANT-PARENT COMPANY RELATEDNESS TYPE

1. Marketing: at least 75% of sales in the first two years from either previous immediate or end customers of the parent company. Businesses obtaining 50–75% of sales from previous customers should be assigned to marketing only if they fail to meet rules 2 and 3.
2. Technology: entrant reports benefits from either product or process knowledge.
3. Forward integration: 20% or more of purchases obtained from other components of the parent company.
4. Conglomerate: entrants not meeting any of rules 1–3.

Rules for Assigning Entrants Not Meeting More Than One of Rules 1–3

5. If entrant reports 75% or more of sales from previous customers and benefits from product or process knowledge, assign to marketing if it also reports benefits from parent company marketing programs or brand names; otherwise, assign to joint relatedness (rule 8).
6. If entrant reports 75% or more of sales from previous customers and 20% or more of purchases obtained internally, assign to marketing if it also reports benefits from parent company marketing programs or brand names and percentage purchases is less than 40% (midpoint of the 20–80% range); otherwise assign to joint relatedness (rule 8).
7. If entrant reports product or process knowledge benefits and more than 20% of purchases obtained internally, assign to forward integration if the percentage of purchases is 40% or higher; otherwise assign to joint relatedness (rule 8).
8. If rules 5 and 6 and follow-up questioning of managers, where possible, do not clarify cases of joint relatedness, assign entrant to joint relatedness group.

The performance impact of the conglomerate and joint types of relatedness is not presented because of small sample sizes for these subpopulations.

RELATEDNESS-PERFORMANCE HYPOTHESES

It will be recalled from chapter 2 that relatedness stands for the functional skill or skills, if any, that an entrant inherits from its parent company and attempts to transfer to a product-market where the parent has not previously competed. The different types of relatedness endow an entrant business with different strengths and weaknesses, and it is argued here that this initial inheritance or skill endowment affects its performance by affecting the type and magnitude of the task[6] it faces as it seeks to become established. But the different types of relatedness also mean that the parent company employees have varying degrees of familiarity with the functional skills needed to become established in the entered market. Thus, an entrant business, from the nature of its relatedness to its parent, not only has some weaknesses but also lacks executive skills to overcome them. For example, a forward integration business might not have marketing channels in the entered market and, at the same time, not have a core of executives who understand, say, mass-merchandisers. The result is difficulty in implementing a key functional skill and, probably, higher operating ratios and lower financial and market performance. This argument is illustrated in figure 5 and expanded below as specific hypotheses are developed.

Hypotheses about Forward Integration Entrants

Forward integration entrants, by definition and according to the data, draw little or no sales and product or

---

6. It is recognized that other factors also affect the task facing an entrant business. For example, an entrant with an incremental innovation may face difficulties in persuading customers to change to its product and in perfecting the production process, both of which raise costs. Some of the other factors are discussed later in this chapter for each type of relatedness.

FIGURE 5. TYPE OF RELATEDNESS: EFFECTS ON ENTRANT BUSINESS PERFORMANCE

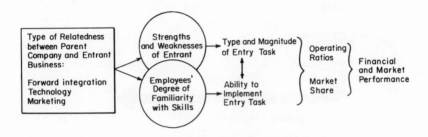

process knowledge from their parent company in their first two years of commercialization. Indeed, this type of entrant is now in competition with the parent's previous customers, and its employees must learn the needs of a customer group at least two levels away from the parent's traditional level of operations in the industry. The plastics industry provides a practical example of their situation. Figure 6 shows the five stages of plastics production. The initial stages, labeled monomers and polymers, entail the preparation of building-block chemicals. These chemicals are then converted into intermediate or end-user products through the stages of compounding, processing, and fabrication.

There is a difference between the task requirements and skill familiarity required at the first two stages and the latter three stages. Monomers and polymers require chemical skills and the abilities to produce a standardized and consistent product in large quantities, at low margins. Capital needs for plant, R&D applications, and marketing to a wide variety of industries are usually key. In direct contrast, the conversion levels require physical and mechanical skills, differentiated products, and smaller "made-to-

FIGURE 6. LEVELS OF PRODUCTION, TASK REQUIREMENTS, AND SKILL
FAMILIARITY IN THE PLASTICS INDUSTRY

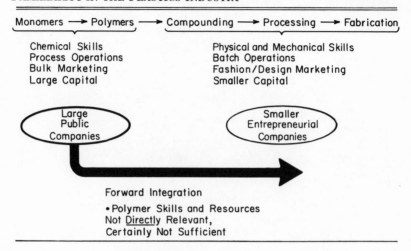

order" production runs. In at least partial response to these
requirements, the industrial structure at the initial stages
consists of a few large firms with access to capital and the
ability to organize multifunctional operations. At the conversion stages, the structure is much more competitive
because the capital requirements are smaller; the organization task is less critical but specialty expertise in a process or application for a particular industry is much more
critical.

The large absolute-size monomer and polymer firms frequently integrate forward. However, instead of marketing
to compounders, these firms now market to, say, processors
and are in competition with their former customers, the
compounders. The large public chemical firms' employees
must now learn the job of the compounder and how to
compete against them, as well as the needs of the processors and how to market to them. They must develop a
customer base, set up a marketing system and learn the
R&D and manufacturing processes appropriate to the new
product market. This list amounts to a formidable task and
yet existing skills in chemicals, process production, and
bulk marketing are not directly relevant to implementing
this task and are certainly not sufficient. It seems likely,
therefore, that forward integration entrants will be an im-

portant source of the large manufacturing, R&D, and marketing to sales ratios reported for the whole sample in chapter 4.

The task specified for forward integration entrants also requires investment in new facilities and marketing programs. However, the entrant business is based on an input or on hardware produced and marketed by the parent company. This association may lower the absolute size of investments needed to commence operations. These linkages suggest that the capital structure ratios of forward integration entrants will show no unusual values: that is, they will be close to the median and mean values for the sample as a whole.

Predicting the relative market share performance of forward integration entrants is difficult. Because the entrant business is in the same industry as the parent, and may in fact have been started to stimulate parent company demand or obtain more value added, it may attain a large share fairly early. On the other hand, some forward integration businesses are launched to give the parent nominal representation in the forward market or to sell only that output that the parent's regular customers cannot absorb.[7] In these cases, market share would be low. As a result of this conflict, no predictions about forward integration market performance will be made.

Hypotheses about Technology Entrants

Technology related entrants, by the definition used here, also draw little or no sales from previous customers of the parent company. Thus, in common with forward integration entrants, they too must develop a customer base and set up a marketing system. Again, however, parent company employees will not be familiar enough with the skills required in the entered product-market to be able to develop a market quickly. They have launched the business because their proprietary product or process

---

7. These considerations suggest that if one knew the parent company objectives, market share could be partially predicted. Unfortunately, as noted in chapter 1, parent company objectives were found in field work to be uncertain and rarely articulated *ex ante*.

knowledge can assist customers in a product-market where the parent company has not previously competed. Thus, they are familiar with their technology but not with the task of transferring it. This fact leads to the expectation that just about all operating and capital structure ratios will be high for technology entrants.

Parent companies in the electrical and electronic fields are frequent launchers of entrants with a technology type of relatedness. An illustration of their task, and their strengths and weaknesses, is provided by a company with technological skills in high vacuum tubes, electromagnetic techniques, and particle physics. This company launched a business to enter the medical x-ray product-market with an improved diagnostic tube. The employees had no knowledge of the medical market and no practical manufacturing experience with diagnostic x-ray tubes. The parent's new business had to install new facilities; overcome start-up manufacturing problems; find out the buying process in hospitals; educate doctors, administrators, nurses, and physicists about the new method of making tubes and its costs and benefits; and plan an after-sales service program.

This example suggests that technology entrants face a formidable task. Their situation is further worsened by the likelihood that initial sales of the substitute technology or method will be low. Thus, large absolute expenditures on manufacturing, marketing, R&D, and facilities are being made at a time when the denominator in their operating and capital ratios is low, absolutely. It seems probable, therefore, that, along with forward integration entrants, technology entrants will be an important source of the large operating ratios reported in chapter 4. Furthermore, as they are applying knowledge in a product-market new to the parent, it seems unlikely that any benefits can be obtained from existing facilities. This characteristic should lead to technology entrants' having the highest investment-to-sales ratio among the three types of relatedness.

As well as being pessimistic about technology entrants' financial performance, it would also seem appropriate to expect a market performance below the sample average. Apart from the probability that all the problems enumerated above will limit initial sales revenues, it also seems likely that the penetration rate of their substitute method will be slow. Buyers need time to change, both to exhaust existing inventory and to satisfy themselves about the suitability and efficacy of the technology entrant's offering.

Hypotheses about Marketing Entrants

Marketing related entrants, by definition and according to the data, draw a substantial portion of their first two years' sales from existing customers of their parent company. Accordingly, parent company executives should be familiar with the distribution, selling, and promotional practices in the entered market. Conversely, given that the product and technology are new to them, marketing entrants may experience some manufacturing and R&D problems. On balance, it is probable that marketing entrants can generate sales revenues more quickly than the other two types of entrant. They possess clear advantages on the demand side and their problems on the supply side are likely to be less severe. They are unlikely to be entering with a substitute technology—which, it has been suggested, inhibits technology entrants' initial sales. And their familiarity with their initial customer groups should have given them a greater awareness of the type of product performance needed and how they will deliver what the market requires. Indeed, marketing entrants, on the manufacturing and R&D side of their business, may do no more than imitate incumbents and rely on superior marketing access or ability to penetrate the entered product market. The example of Xerox in chapter 2 is illustrative of marketing entry selling a similar product and relying on existing customer relationships. Gillette's entry into the felt-tip pen product-market and John Deere's entry into snowmobiles are other examples.

These considerations lead to the view that the task facing marketing entrants is less formidable than that facing forward integration and technology entrants. Furthermore, employees of parent companies launching marketing entrants are likely to possess more familiarity with the functional skills needed to compete in the entered product-markets. They are inherently more familiar with marketing skills and, if they enter later in the product life cycle than, say, technology entrants, they will have been able to study designs and processes used by others. The combination of an easier task and greater ability to implement it should ease marketing entrants' absolute expenditures, and their quicker absolute sales generation would provide larger denominators in their operating and capital structure ratios. The result is an expectation that entrants with the marketing type of relatedness will perform considerably better than the sample mean and median ratios.

The foregoing discussion of the strengths and weaknesses of each type of relatedness and the degree of familiarity with the functional skills required to compete in the entered product-market provides the basis for some testable hypotheses. These hypotheses are summarized below. The first four hypotheses deal with the expected association between type of relatedness and degree of familiarity with functional skills. The next three deal with relatedness and operating and capital ratios. The final two predict performance in the first two years of commercialization.

Hypotheses: *Relatedness and Skill Familiarity*

1. The degree of familiarity of parent company executives with the manufacturing skills required in the entered product-market will be lowest for forward integration and technology related entrants.
2. Familiarity with R&D skills will be higher for technology related entrants than for the other two types.
3. Familiarity with marketing skills will be higher for marketing entrants than the other two types of relatedness.
4. Familiarity with finance skills will be similar for all three types of entrant.

Hypotheses: *Relatedness and Performance*

5. Forward integration and technology entrants will report the most negative financial performance in the first two years of entry.

6. Technology entrants will report the lowest relative market share and marketing entrants the highest relative market share in the first two years of entry.

Hypotheses: *Relatedness and Operating Capital Structure Ratios*

7. Forward integration and technology entrants will report the highest manufacturing/sales, R&D/sales and marketing/sales operating ratios in the first two years of entry.
8. Technology entrants will report the highest investment/sales capital structure ratio in the first two years of entry.
9. Marketing entrants will report the lowest ratios on all operating and capital structure ratios during the first two years.

TESTING RELATEDNESS-PERFORMANCE HYPOTHESES

Testing Hypotheses about Skill Familiarity

Data for testing the hypotheses on skill familiarity were obtained by asking managers to rate the degree of familiarity of parent company executives, at the time the entrant business commenced operations, with the skills needed to compete in the entered product-market. A 3-point rating scheme was used where 1 stood for "very unfamiliar," 2 for "some familiarity," and 3 for "very familiar"; answers were treated as a ratio-scale variable. Some caution should be used in interpreting the answers, however, because the question called for a managerial perception ex post. For example, the answers could reflect, at least partially, managers' actual difficulties with the different skills in the entered market rather than, as requested, their perception of their strengths and weaknesses at the time of entry.

At the request of managers interviewed during preliminary field work, the marketing skill was broken down into three separate skills: "distribution methods," "selling methods," and "marketing practices" (covering pricing and promotion and product policy). Thus, the question called for perceptions of familiarity with six functional skills—the three marketing skills and manufacturing, R&D, and finance skills. No separate hypotheses were developed for distribution, selling, and marketing practices.

The mean scores for the three types of relatedness and skill familiarity are shown in table 26. In general, the direction of the differences are in accord with the hypotheses above. Hypothesis 1, that forward integration and technology entrants will report the lowest familiarity with manufacturing, is not rejected. Hypothesis 2, that technology entrants will report the highest familiarity with R&D, is also not rejected. Hypothesis 4, that familiarity with financial skills will not vary by type of relatedness, is similarly not rejected.

On the other hand, hypothesis 3, that marketing entrants will report the highest familiarity with marketing skills, is not supported. There is no significant difference among forward integration, technology, and marketing entrants on familiarity with marketing practices (pricing and promotion and product policy), as illustrated by the mean scores of 2.29, 2.20 and 2.27, respectively. On selling methods, marketing entrants reported a mean familiarity of 2.36, while forward integration reported 2.00—a difference of 0.36. There is, however, a 16 percent chance that the difference between the true subpopulation means will have a sign opposite from that between these two sample means. On distribution methods, marketing entrants reported 2.55 while forward integration entrants reported 2.14 and technology entrants reported 2.10. Again, although the direction is as expected, the probability levels indicate the need for caution.

Also shown in table 26 is the combined familiarity with all six skills, expressed as a percentage of the maximum potential familiarity. Thus, a score of 100 percent on this index indicates that the parent company executives were considered very familiar with each of the six skills at the time of entry. Forward integration entrants reported the lowest degree of familiarity, with 65 percent, while technology entrants reported 71 percent and marketing entrants reported the highest, with 77 percent. Median index

TABLE 26. TYPE OF RELATEDNESS AND MEAN DEGREE OF FAMILIARITY WITH FUNCTIONAL SKILLS IN THE ENTERED PRODUCT-MARKET

	Type of Relatedness			
Functional Skill	Forward Integration (n = 7)	Technology (n = 10)	Marketing (n = 11)[a]	Probability Level of Significance Tests[b]
Manufacturing technology	1.7 (0.49)[c]	1.6 (0.70)	2.27 (0.79)	Marketing vs. other two = 0.03
Research and development	1.57 (0.54)	2.6 (0.70)	2.09 (0.70)	Technology vs. forward integration = 0.00 Technology vs. marketing = 0.07 Marketing vs. forward integration = 0.06
Distribution methods	2.14 (0.90)	2.10 (0.74)	2.55 (0.52)	Technology vs. marketing = 0.08
Selling methods	2.00 (0.58)	2.20 (0.92)	2.36 (0.81)	Forward integration vs. marketing = 0.17
Marketing practices[d]	2.29 (0.76)	2.20 (0.63)	2.27 (0.79)	Forward integration vs. marketing = 0.16
Financial practices	2.57 (0.54)	2.50 (0.53)	2.55 (0.52)	
Index[e] of skill familiarity	65% (14)	71% (18)	77% (14)	Forward integration vs. marketing = 0.06

[a] One marketing entrant out of twelve identified did not provide data on skill familiarity.

[b] Assuming unequal variances, the mean for each type of relatedness is tested against the other two in turn. Tests not shown when probability level exceeds 0.2.

[c] Residual standard deviation.

[d] Pricing and promotion and product policy.

[e] Constructed by: $\sum_{i=1}^{6} \left(\dfrac{\text{Reported familiarity with skill}_i}{6 \times 3 \ (= \text{very familiar})} \right) \times 100$.

readings are 67 percent, 73 percent, and 80 percent for the three types respectively.

Testing Hypotheses about Operating, Capital, and Performance Ratios

Hypothesis 5 on performance is not reflected by the data. Marketing entrants recorded the best financial performance in the first two years of entry, outperforming the other two on all financial performance measures (see table 27). For example, median ROI was -20 percent for marketing entrants, -52 percent for technology entrants, and -93 percent for forward integration entrants. On most financial measures, technology and forward integration entrants were significantly inferior to marketing entrants.

Market performance in table 27 is difficult to interpret because marketing entrants had the lowest mean relative market share, at 23 percent, but the highest median relative market share, at 14 percent. Several outliers influenced the mean relative share for technology and forward integration entrant and I judged that the median is a better statistic. Under this interpretation, median share data do not refute hypothesis 6 for marketing entrants.

Hypotheses 7, 8, and 9 on operating and capital ratios are not generally rejected, as shown in table 28. Forward integration and technology entrants do exhibit the highest ratios on manufacturing/sales, R&D/sales, and marketing/sales ratios. The differences between mean pairs are significant at 0.06 or better, except for manufacturing/sales ratio where the probability level is 0.15. Median manufacturing ratios indicate that forward integration entrants, at 35 percent, experienced the highest manufacturing/sales ratio, while technology and marketing entrants were similar, at 27 percent and 28 percent respectively. Technology entrants reported monumental R&D/sales ratio with mean 95 percent and median 102 percent; presumably this reflects both the costs of transferring technology and the low initial sales of a substitute method discussed earlier. Forward integration entrants recorded the highest marketing/sales ratio at 76 percent. This finding would seem to be eloquent evidence of the marketing

TABLE 27. OPERATING AND CAPITAL STRUCTURE RATIOS BY TYPE OF RELATEDNESS, FIRST TWO YEARS

Percentage Operating Ratios		Type of Relatedness			Probability Levels
		Forward Integration (n = 7)	Technology (n = 10)	Marketing (n = 12)	
Purchasing/sales	Mean	51	45	45	
	Median	52	46	43	
Manufacturing/sales[a]	Mean	51	43	28	Forward integration vs. marketing = 0.15
	Median	35	27	28	
R&D/sales	Mean	54	95	12	Technology vs. marketing = 0.02
	Median	63	102	5	Forward integration vs. marketing = 0.05
Marketing/sales	Mean	74	50	26	Forward integration vs. marketing = 0.06
	Median	76	54	23	Technology vs. marketing = 0.01
Percentage Capital Structure Ratios					
Receivables/sales	Mean	15	21	15	
	Median	13	17	13	
Inventory/sales[a]	Mean	46	55	26	Technology vs. marketing = 0.14
	Median	63	28	27	
Investment/sales	Mean	121	444	76	Forward integration vs. technology = 0.16 Forward integration vs. marketing = 0.06
	Median	117	152	80	Technology vs. marketing = 0.14

[a] Two service businesses excluded from forward integration subpopulation sample.

TABLE 28. PERFORMANCE MEASURES BY TYPE OF RELATEDNESS, FIRST TWO YEARS

Percentage Major Measures		Type of Relatedness			Probability Levels (Greater Than 0.2 Not Shown)
		Forward Integration (n = 7)	Technology (n = 10)	Marketing (n = 12)	
Cash flow/investment	Mean	-115	-122	-76	Marketing vs. technology = 0.04
($R^2 = 0.10$)	Median	-135	-91	-76	Marketing vs. forward integration = 0.06
Return on investment	Mean	-94	-112	-22	Marketing vs. forward integration = 0.04
($R^2 = 0.12$)	Median	-93	-52	-20	Marketing vs. technology = 0.03
Return on sales	Mean	-133	-159	-20	Marketing vs. forward integration = 0.05
($R^2 = 0.20$)	Median	-79	-103	-10	Marketing vs. technology = 0.01
Relative market share	Mean	36[a]	38	23	
($R^2 = 0.14$)	Median	2	4	14	

[a] n = 6 because of incomplete market data on one business.

difficulties anticipated for forward integration entrants. Technology entrants recorded the next highest marketing/sales ratio, median 54 percent, while marketing entrants again showed the lowest ratio, with 23 percent. Study of the capital structure ratio in table 27 shows that technology entrants had the highest median investment/ sales ratio at 152 percent, compared with forward integration entrants at 117 percent and marketing entrants at 80 percent.

THE SECOND TWO YEARS

The above study of the first two years naturally leads to the question whether the differences in performance among the types of relatedness continued to hold in the third and fourth years of entry. Unfortunately, study of this question is handicapped by small sample sizes. The sample of forward integration entrants is reduced to five in the third and fourth years, and that of marketing entrants to eight. The technology sample is also reduced to five and suffers a further complication in that one of them is an outlier that distorts the mean estimates for this type of entrant on most of the ratios. For these reasons, discussion in this section will focus on median performance. No hypotheses were formulated for the second two years because the impact of relatedness will have been diluted in unpredictable ways owing to organizational learning and, presumably, competitive reaction to entry.

Forward integration entrants continued to report the lowest ROI performance in the second two years. Table 29 shows that their median ROI was −68 percent, compared with −17 percent for technology entrants and −5 percent for marketing entrants. On cash flow/investment, however, they shared the lowest performance, at −34 percent, with technology entrants; marketing entrants reported −19 percent. At the same time, forward integration entrants performed worse than technology and marketing entrants on median relative market share.

Not surprisingly, in view of the performance recorded above, forward integration entrants reported the largest

TABLE 29. OPERATING AND CAPITAL STRUCTURE RATIOS BY
TYPE OF RELATEDNESS, SECOND TWO YEARS

Percentage Operating Ratios		*Type of Relatedness*		
		Forward Integration (n = 5)	*Technology (n = 5)*	*Marketing (n = 8)*
Purchasing/sales	Mean	63	43	47
	Median	62	40	44
Manufacturing/sales	Mean	—[a]	28	26
	Median	—	28	30
R&D/sales	Mean	20	55	6
	Median	24	15	3
Marketing/sales	Mean	23	45	20
	Median	23	24	20
Percentage Capital Structure Ratios				
Receivables/sales	Mean	13	26	15
	Median	12	23	13
Inventory/sales	Mean	—	160	26
	Median	—	31	31
Investment/sales	Mean	63	650	65
	Median	49	87	57

[a] Not shown because exclusion of two service businesses reduces subpopulation sample size to three.

operating ratios, as shown in table 30. For example, these entrants showed a median 62 percent on purchases/sales, compared with 40 percent for technology entrants and 44 percent for marketing entrants. They took over the highest position on R&D/sales ratios from technology entrants, reporting a median of 24 percent compared with 15 percent for technology entrants and 3 percent for marketing entrants. They reported 23 percent on marketing/sales, about the same as the 24 percent for technology entrants; marketing entrants reported 20 percent. On the other hand, the data suggest that forward integration entrants have the lowest capital structure ratios. Their median investment/sales ratio was 49 percent, almost half the 87 percent recorded by technology entrants and slightly lower than the 57 percent for marketing entrants.

TABLE 30. PERFORMANCE MEASURES BY TYPE OF
RELATEDNESS, SECOND TWO YEARS

Percentage *Major Measures*		*Forward* *Integration* *(n = 5)*	*Technology* *(n = 5)*	*Marketing* *(n = 8)*
Cash flow/investment	Mean	−60	−51	−25
($R^2 = 0.06$)	Median	−34	−34	−19
ROI	Mean	−63	−35	−14
($R^2 = 0.04$)	Median	−68	−17	−5
Return on sales	Mean	−29	−113	−8
($R^2 = 0.15$)	Median	−31	−35	−2
Relative market share	Mean	20	20	31
($R^2 = 0.16$)	Median	5	12	14
Relative price/cost (1.0 = same as competitors)	Mean	0.89	0.85	1.02
($R^2 = 0.21$)	Median	0.95	0.90	0.97

It seems that forward integration entrants are still experiencing difficulties. Conversely, technology entrants have shown considerable improvement in operations, but are still plagued by large investment/sales ratios. Of course, it is possible that the true performance of forward integration entrants is not revealed in their own income statements and balance sheets. The parent company could be taking a loss in the forward business as a means of protecting or enhancing a profit elsewhere in the line. The unusually high purchase/sales ratio of 62 percent mentioned above could be one indication of this practice. Lacking fuller information on individual parent company policies, it can only be noted here that entrants with a forward integration type of relatedness perform less well than marketing entrants in the first four years and less well than technology entrants in the second two years. Individual managers of forward integration entrants would have to check that profits elsewhere in the line are sufficient to compensate for the magnitude of losses seen in this study. Similar caution is not needed in evaluating relative share performance: there is little doubt in concluding that forward integration entrants exhibited the lowest relative share in the first four years of entry.

8. The Impact of Market Characteristics on Performance

THIS CHAPTER IS CONCERNED with the impact on entrants' performance of the characteristics of the entered product-market. The method of analysis is, first, to study performance in the first two years of entry according to a static description of the market as it existed at the time of entry. These descriptions are based on the stage of product category life cycle and the number of sellers combined with the level of concentration. The second analysis studies the impact on average performance in the first four years of different growth rates in the entered market.

PERFORMANCE AND MARKET TYPES

The conceptual scheme in chapter 2 linked the product category life cycle model to market structure models to obtain a classification of market types. It was argued there that monopoly would be most common in the introductory stage of the life cycle, monopolistic competition or oligopoly in the growth stage, and oligopoly in the mature stage. The verification of this classification is now undertaken empirically.

Managers were asked to judge the stage of development of the product category at the time their business entered the market. Of the entrants studied, 28 percent entered in the introductory stage, 57 percent in the growth stage, and 15 percent in the mature stage; no business in this sample entered a product-market in the decline stage (see table 31).

Managers were also asked to estimate the number of businesses in the product-market and the market shares of the top four in the year prior to their entry. Of the forty entrants, thirty-four were able to provide complete information (see table 32). The number of businesses and the share held by the top four were combined in a manner similar to Bain's proposed gradation in oligopoly (1968: 134–144). This sample was divided into three groups, retaining Bain's type 1, merging types 2 and 3, and retaining type 4. The first group, called "tight oligopoly," referred to entered product-market structures consisting of fewer than five businesses and with the top four sharing 75 percent or more of total product-market sales. This group included the four monopolies that were entered. The combination of types 2 and 3, called "moderate oligopoly," referred to product-markets with more than five competitors and with the top four sharing between 55 and 74 percent of total sales. The third group, called "loose oligopoly" and designed similarly to Bain's type 4, referred

TABLE 31. STAGE OF PRODUCT CATEGORY LIFE CYCLE AT
TIME OF ENTRY

Stage	Number of Entrants	Percentage of Entrants
Introductory: primary demand just starting; many potential users unfamiliar with products.	11	28
Growth: real growth 10% or more; technology and/or competitive structure still changing.	23	57
Maturity: potential users familiar with products; technology and competitive structure stable.	6	15
Decline: products viewed as commodities; weaker competitors existing.	0	0
	40	100

TABLE 32. NUMBER OF BUSINESSES AND TOP FOUR MARKET SHARES, YEAR PRIOR TO ENTRY

Number of Businesses	Number of Entrants	Percentage of Entrants	Top Four Market Shares	Number of Entrants	Percentage of Entrants
1	4	11	100–90%	13	38
2–5	12	39	89–75%	5	15
6–15	8	24	74–55%	9	26
16–30	7	18	Less than 55%	7	21
More than 30	3	8			
	34	100		34	100

to product-markets with more than five businesses and with the top four sharing less than 55 percent of total sales. Of the thirty-four entrants studied on this question, fifteen entered tight oligopolies (including monopolies), twelve entered moderate oligopolies, and seven entered loose oligopolies.

In table 33, the product category life cycle stages of the entered markets are combined in a matrix with the market structures. Examination of these data reveals that these two models of markets cannot be combined in the straightforward manner envisaged in chapter 2. According to this sample, a particular market structure is not more likely than another to appear at a certain stage in the product category life cycle, although the monopoly structure does, presumably, characterize the start of a new industry. Consequently, because these two aspects of markets are not combinable, their impacts on entrant performance must be analyzed separately.

LIFE CYCLE–PERFORMANCE HYPOTHESIS

The stage in the product category life cycle is meant to be a proxy for the market's growth rate and the extent to which the market is developed on the demand side and on manufacturing technology. To check the first characteristic, managers were asked to estimate the average annual growth rate of the value of total shipments in the three years *prior* to the year of their entry. The expectation is

TABLE 33. PRODUCT CATEGORY LIFE CYCLE AND TYPE OF OLIGOPOLY MODELS FOR ENTERED MARKETS

	Tight Oligopoly	Moderate Oligopoly	Loose Oligopoly	Total
Introductory stage (1 monopoly)	3	3	3	9
Growth stage (3 monopolies)	10	7	4	21
Maturity stage	2	2	0	4
Total	15	12	7	34

that the growth stage should show the highest growth rate and the mature stage the lowest. The estimates showed that the growth stage did in fact have the highest growth rate (see table 34), although there is practically no difference between the median 15 percent rate for that stage and 13 percent for the introductory stage. There seems to be little doubt that mature markets with a median of 3 percent had the lowest growth rate.

We may speculate that, in general, entrants into product-markets in the growth stage face a number of initial advantages over those entering either the introductory or mature stages. First, risks are lower because the initial act of innovation has occurred; uncertainty about market acceptance and manufacturing technology, although probably still acute, is easing. Second, demand is still price-elastic, whereas it may be inelastic in maturity. Third, volume should be easier to obtain because the entrant can appeal to new customers rather than to the current customers of the incumbent businesses. Fourth, the differential costs between entrants and the incumbents should not yet be severe. Finally, if the product is not yet a commodity but the market is mature, it is likely that buyer loyalties exist toward the incumbent businesses, thus raising barriers to entry. That is, because the product is older it is more likely that alternate ways of differentiating the product have already been tried. Thus, the marginal cost of product differentiation strategies rises through the life cycle and is higher for later entrants than for earlier entrants.

In short, entrants in the introductory stage face a market

TABLE 34. ANNUAL PRE-ENTRY GROWTH RATE BY STAGE OF
PRODUCT CATEGORY LIFE CYCLE

Percentage Annual Growth Rate	Introductory Stage (n = 11)	Growth Stage (n = 23)	Mature Stage (n = 6)	Probability Level
Mean	13	42	5	Mature vs. introductory = 0.03
(Standard deviation)	(8)	(75)	(6)	
Median	13	15	3	

development task and those in the mature stage face a market penetration task. These two tasks are likely to result in higher operating and capital ratios, and inferior financial performance, than for those entering the growth stage because the latter benefit from market momentum.

For example, entrants into the growth stage should have lower marketing/sales and R&D/sales ratios than entrants into markets in the introductory stage. First, the more advanced stage of market development should lessen their absolute dollar expenditures on developing products and markets, and second, the absolute sales revenues should be higher in the growth stage. Similarly, it seems likely that their relative direct costs will be lower. Entrants into the growth stage should also have lower marketing/sales and R&D/sales ratios than entrants into markets in the mature stage. The low growth rate characteristic of the mature stage means that entrants' sales must be won directly from incumbents. The marketing and R&D costs of sufficiently differentiating themselves from these incumbents so as to break any existing buyer loyalties are likely to be high. It is also possible that these more difficult entry conditions will cause initial absolute sales revenues to be low, thus further worsening their operating ratios.

It seems likely that these same considerations would also produce the lowest investment ratios for entrants into the growth stage. Entrants into the introductory stage face relatively small demand, yet must build a plant adequate to handle later demand and obtain minimum efficient scale. It is not so clear, however, that entrants into the mature stage will have higher investment ratios. Much will depend on the particular characteristics of the product-market entered.

In contrast to the expectation that entrants into the growth stage will show superior financial performance, it is probable that entrants into the introductory stage will show superior relative share performance. This hypothesis arises simply from the fact of their earlier entrance into the product-market.

Table 35 shows that the most one can say is that the data point to the support of these expectations but not in a statistically convincing manner. The most negative finan-

TABLE 35. OPERATING AND CAPITAL STRUCTURE RATIOS BY PRODUCT OR SERVICE CATEGORY LIFE CYCLE, FIRST TWO YEARS

Percentage Operating Ratios		*Product Category Life Cycle*			*Probability Levels (above 0.2 Not Shown)*
		Introductory Stage (n = 11)	*Growth Stage (n = 23)*	*Mature Stage (n = 6)*	
Purchasing/sales	Mean	47	47	44	
	Median	41	46	50	
Manufacturing/sales[a]	Mean	37	43	29	
	Median	27	41	10	
R&D/sales	Mean	51	38	47	
	Median	43	11	112	
Marketing/sales	Mean	44	37	47	Growth vs. mature = 0.17
	Median	40	31	40	
Percentage Capital Structure Ratios					
Receivables/sales	Mean	20	16	17	
	Median	17	13	15	
Inventory/sales[a]	Mean	61	30	18	
	Median	40	29	12	
Investment/sales	Mean	420	116	232	Introductory vs. growth = 0.15
	Median	109	89	166	

[a] Three service businesses excluded.

cial performance for the first two years of entry tends to occur among those entrants who entered in the mature stage. Also as expected, entrants into the introductory stage showed the highest relative market share. However, a general note of caution must be sounded. The differences among the means can only be taken as suggestive. In all cases, the subsample standard deviations remained high— much higher, for example, than those found in chapter 7 when the sample was divided into types of relatedness. Furthermore, the R^2 are extremely low. The medians do tend to behave as expected—most negative on financial performance in the introductory and mature stages and highest on relative share in the introductory stage. After considering all the evidence, it seems that caution in interpretation of these data is advisable. It is surprising that the differences in performance according to stage of entry are not more marked.

Similarly, expectations on operating and capital ratios are supported by the data but not strongly. For example, table 36 shows that the mean and median R&D/sales ratios are considerably higher for entrants into the mature and introductory stages. There is, however, a 17 percent chance that the sign on the differences between the growth and mature means could be reversed. Studying means and medians, it is apparent that marketing/sales ratios also follow the expected pattern. The manufacturing/sales ratios exhibit puzzling behavior. Both the mean and the median are highest in the growth stage, whereas one might have expected this result in the introductory stage, given the higher probability of doubt about manufacturing technology in this stage. Manufacturing/sales is lowest in the mature stage. This result could be explained by the possibility that manufacturing technology is more settled in the mature stage.

Of the capital ratios, the investment/sales mean and median are highest in the introductory and mature stage. Mean investment/sales in both stages is influenced by a few large outliers which illustrate that the capital side of developing or penetrating a market can also be severe. Although the subsample is small, it seems fair to point out that these outliers in the introductory stage entered proc-

TABLE 36. PERFORMANCE MEASURES BY PRODUCT CATEGORY LIFE CYCLE STAGE, FIRST TWO YEARS

Percentage Major Measures		*Product Category Life Cycle Stage*			*Probability Levels (above 0.2 Not Shown)*
		Introductory Stage (n = 11)	*Growth Stage (n = 23)*	*Mature Stage (n = 6)*	
Cash flow/investment	Mean	-90	-103	-126	
(R² = 0.04)	Median	-81	-76	-93	
Return on investment	Mean	50	-77	-133	Introductory vs. mature = 0.19
(R² = 0.06)	Median	32	-39	-53	
Return on sales	Mean	-96	-77	-146	
(R² = 0.04)	Median	-53	-30	-91	
Relative market share	Mean	84	24	47	Introductory vs. growth = 0.02
(R² = 0.01)	Median	58	11	20	

ess product-markets, presumably subject to large indivisibilities of plant investment. The inventory/sales ratio
exhibits interesting behavior—declining from a mean of
61 percent in the introductory stage to 30 percent in the
growth stage and to 18 percent in the mature stage. Again,
it is probable that, as with manufacturing, more stable
market conditions enabled entrants into mature markets to
better predict factory sales and, therefrom, material and
finished good requirements.

OLIGOPOLY TYPE–PERFORMANCE HYPOTHESIS

It seems best to move straight to the data to see the
impact of oligopoly type on performance because of the
general indeterminacy of the oligopoly structure. One can
argue that a loose oligopoly would be easier to enter because incumbents are less likely to be directly affected by
the addition of an extra supplier. On the other hand, as
Bain has suggested (1968: 142), a loose oligopoly may
perform much like an atomistic structure. In this case,
there would be less above normal profits for the entrant.
A tight oligopoly might, if joint profit maximization existed,
offer higher profits to the entrant, but it is uncertain, ex
ante, whether the entrant would be allowed into the group.
Another consideration is the extent to which the type of
oligopoly is a proxy for severity of entry barriers. It is
probable that a loose oligopoly has lower entry barriers
than a tight oligopoly. In this case, one would expect superior financial performance from entrants into the loose
structure. At the same time, the greater number of competitors and lower concentration means that each incumbent has a low absolute share of market. Therefore, an
entrant could find it easier to obtain a larger relative share
in the loose oligopoly structure than in the tight oligopoly
structure.

Table 37 shows that the performance varied significantly
according to the type of market structure entered. Entrants
into loose oligopolies show consistently less negative financial performance on all measures. To take just one
example, median return on sales was −11 percent in loose

TABLE 37. OPERATING AND CAPITAL STRUCTURE RATIOS BY TYPE OF OLIGOPOLY ENTERED, FIRST TWO YEARS

Percentage Operating Ratios		Tight Oligopoly (n = 15)	Moderate Oligopoly (n = 12)	Loose Oligopoly (n = 7)	Probability Levels (above 0.2 Not Shown)
Purchasing/sales	Mean	44	40	60	Moderate oligopoly vs. loose oligopoly = 0.04
	Median	40	35	56	Tight oligopoly vs. loose oligopoly = 0.08
Manufacturing/sales[a]	Mean	42	36	24	Tight oligopoly vs. loose oligopoly = 0.07
	Median	26	27	27	
R&D/sales	Mean	70	23	21	Tight oligopoly vs. loose oligopoly = 0.06
	Median	46	12	1	Tight oligopoly vs. moderate oligopoly = 0.04
Marketing/sales	Mean	55	36	17	Tight oligopoly vs. loose oligopoly = 0.01
	Median	41	39	12	Tight oligopoly vs. moderate oligopoly = 0.07
					Moderate oligopoly vs. loose oligopoly = 0.06
Percentage Capital Structure Ratios					
Receivables/sales	Mean	16	20	15	
	Median	13	17	15	
Inventory/sales[a]	Mean	29	35	68	Tight oligopoly vs. loose oligopoly = 0.16
	Median	26	31	31	
Investment/sales	Mean	118	120	581	Tight oligopoly vs. loose oligopoly = 0.18
	Median				

[a] Three service businesses excluded.

oligopolies compared to −95 percent in tight oligopolies. Note too that the probability levels on the tests of the mean differences are generally significant by classical norms. Also, the R^2 are much higher in table 37, indicating that the type of oligopoly entered has more explanatory power than the stage of product life cycle entered. This insight is potentially important. For example, it might indicate that entry into a mature market could be successful if it were a loose oligopoly.

Part of the superior performance of entrants into loose oligopolies is explained in table 38. Those entrant business units entering loose oligopolies reported lower marketing/sales and R&D/sales ratios than those entering tight oligopolies. It has already been demonstrated that there is little association between type of market structure and stage of product category life cycle. The explanation of these differences in ratios is, therefore, likely to be associated with some inherent characteristics of the structure. The most plausible is that the tight oligopoly structure is a proxy for more severe barriers to entry. Thus, entrants into this structure had higher operating ratios from both higher absolute expenditures and lower absolute sales revenues.

The general impression from these two analyses is that entry into the introductory and mature stages and a tight oligopoly structure is associated with the highest operating and capital ratios and the most negative financial performance in the first two years. The combination of these stages and a tight oligopoly type would seem to provide a most difficult task for an entrant. Conversely, combining a loose oligopoly structure with either the introductory or mature stages would presumably ameliorate the entry task. Unfortunately, these impressions cannot be tested in this sample because of the small subsample sizes.

MARKET GROWTH–PERFORMANCE HYPOTHESIS

Turning to performance in the first four years of entry, it is appropriate to study the influence on entrant performance of the product-market growth rate. As with type of

TABLE 38. PERFORMANCE MEASURES BY TYPE OF OLIGOPOLY ENTERED, FIRST TWO YEARS

Percentage Performance Measures		Tight Oligopoly (n = 15)	Moderate Oligopoly (n = 12)	Loose Oligopoly (n = 7)	Probability Levels (above 0.2 Not Shown)
Cash flow/investment	Mean	−122	−81	−67	Tight oligopoly vs. loose oligopoly = 0.003
($R^2 = 0.22$)	Median	−117	−81	−61	Tight oligopoly vs. moderate oligopoly = 0.02
					Moderate oligopoly vs. loose oligopoly = 0.03
Return on investment	Mean	−107	−39	−14	Tight oligopoly vs. loose oligopoly = 0.001
($R^2 = 0.21$)	Median	−89	−41	−6	Tight oligopoly vs. moderate oligopoly = 0.02
					Moderate oligopoly vs: loose oligopoly = 0.03
Return on sales	Mean	−126	−50	−43	Tight oligopoly vs. moderate oligopoly = 0.05
($R^2 = 0.14$)	Median	−95	−36	−11	Tight oligopoly vs. loose oligopoly = 0.06
Relative share	Mean	23	35	55	Tight oligopoly vs. loose oligopoly = 0.13
($R^2 = 0.41$)	Median	4	11	13	

oligopoly, it is not clear a priori whether different rates of growth would have a positive or negative influence on entrant business performance. On the one hand, growth could raise short-run product-market profits if its rate is greater than expected by the incumbents and a shortfall in capacity exists. Incumbents, therefore, are reaping windfall profits and the entrant could share these to the extent that its entry capacity, incumbents' capacity additions, and the postentry market growth rate perpetuate the capacity shortfall situation. On the other hand, at least three propositions from business strategy point to growth as a negative influence on short-run profits. First, some strategists believe that their share of market in the future is at least partially dependent on current market share. Second, growth increases the value of share points over the long run. Third, rivals' relative cost position is held to be a function of accumulated volume (Boston Consulting Group 1970). These three points make a case for investing in capacity and other share-gaining activities when product-market growth is rapid. Thus, short-run profits are depressed in the hope of gaining a significant market share and above-normal profits in the long run.

Data in table 39 leave little doubt that superior financial and market performance comes from those entrants into moderate-growth markets. For example, median ROI is -7 percent for entrants into moderate-growth markets but -38 percent for entrants into no-growth markets and -25 percent in high-growth markets. All the other financial measures are least negative for entrants in moderate-growth markets. An interesting finding is that entrants into moderate-growth markets recorded the lowest relative market share. This finding makes their superior financial performance puzzling. An explanation could be their high investment intensity at 402 percent, as shown in table 40: such a high level may indicate high absolute investment outlays which depresses those financial performance measures where investment is in the denominator. This interpretation would mean that moderate growth benefits income statements but penalizes, in the short run, balance sheets. Another interpretation could be that entrants into moderate-growth markets had low R&D and marketing

TABLE 39. OPERATING AND CAPITAL STRUCTURE RATIOS BY ANNUAL PRODUCT-MARKET GROWTH RATE, FIRST FOUR YEARS

Percentage Operating Ratios		No Growth (−30 to +2%) Mean = −7% Median = −3% (n = 8)	Moderate Growth (6 to 20%) Mean = 8% Median = 11% (n = 10)	High Growth (35 to 536%) Mean = 71% Median = 117% (n = 10)	*Probability Levels* (above 0.2 Not Shown)
Purchasing/sales	Mean	50	43	56	
	Median	46	38	49	
Manufacturing/sales[a]	Mean	35	22	49	Moderate growth vs. high growth = 0.04
	Median	39	22	34	No growth vs. high growth = 0.19
					No growth vs. moderate growth = 0.16
R&D/sales	Mean	27	24	27	
	Median	25	6	24	
Marketing/sales	Mean	40	27	22	No growth vs. high growth = 0.03
	Median	33	22	25	No growth vs. moderate growth = 0.15
Percentage Capital Structure Ratios					
Receivables/sales	Mean	13	17	23	
	Median	14	13	18	
Inventory/sales[a]	Mean	28	54	37	No growth vs. moderate growth = 0.19
	Median	30	32	43	
Investment/sales	Mean	75	402	121	No growth vs. moderate growth = 0.15
	Median	66	85	83	

[a] Three service businesses excluded.

TABLE 40. PERFORMANCE MEASURES BY ANNUAL PRODUCT-MARKET GROWTH RATE, FIRST FOUR YEARS

Percentage Performance Measures		*No Growth* (−30 to +2%) *Mean* = −7% *Median* = −3% (n = 8)	*Moderate Growth* (6 to 20%) *Mean* = 8% *Median* = 11% (n = 10)	*High Growth* (35 to 536%) *Mean* = 71% *Median* = 117% (n = 10)	*Probability Levels* (above 0.2 Not Shown)	
Cash flow/investment (R^2 = 0.11)	Mean	−93	−54	−88	Moderate growth vs. no growth	= 0.13
	Median	−69	−42	−84	Moderate growth vs. high growth	= 0.03
Return on investment (R^2 = 0.18)	Mean	−110	−7	−61	No growth vs. moderate growth	= 0.05
	Median	−38	−7	−25	No growth vs. high growth	= 0.02
Return on sales (R^2 = 0.09)	Mean	−56	−40	−39		
	Median	−40	−6	−38		
Relative share (R^2 = 0.12)	Mean	43	13	91	Moderate growth vs. high growth	= 0.03
	Median	13	2	14	No growth vs. high growth	= 0.16

ratios because, as indicated by their low relative market share, they were not attempting an aggressive entry. Data in table 40 show that moderate growth market entrants had the lowest operating ratios. These uncertainties must make any judgments on the impact of market growth on entrant performance highly tentative.

9. The Impact of Entry Strategy on Performance

THIS CHAPTER IS CONCERNED with the impact on performance of the strategy adopted by businesses to commence their operations in the entered product-market. In chapter 2, entry strategy was divided into two parts, posture and marketing mix. Posture covers decisions on whether to offer an incremental innovation or an imitation, the scale of entry, and the degree of integration relative to incumbents. Marketing mix refers to decisions on price, product, length of line, breadth of market segment within the served market, distribution, services and sales force, advertising, and promotion expenditures. Although it was recognized in chapter 2 that these elements of the marketing mix should reinforce one another, it was deemed more practical to develop a classification of mix types based on individual elements. Thus, six types were identified: price cutter, improved quality, broader or specialist product line, market segmentation, improved services, and distribution innovator. The first task in this chapter is to describe how the different elements of posture and mix were measured. Next, the different postures and types of mix in this sample will be identified. Finally, the impact of posture and mix on performance will be analyzed.

MEASURING ENTRY STRATEGY

The method of measuring strategy involved asking executives to compare what their business did against the incumbent businesses. Although relying on opinion, it was hoped that this method would elicit reliable data because the base of comparison—the incumbent businesses—was presumably well known and well defined to the executives. The great obstacle in classifying strategies is that no method has been devised that can compare them across industries and markets. For example, it is not at all clear how one would lay down criteria to identify a market segmentation strategy or a specialist product line strategy in product-markets as diverse as medical electronics, agricultural implements, and cameras. Lacking such criteria, it would be extremely difficult to devise standardized questions about strategies for a broad cross section of businesses and markets. But, by asking the executives to compare themselves against the leading rivals in their served product-market, criteria are no longer needed. Executives simply report whether, for example, their product line was broader, about the same, or narrower than their leading rivals'. The researcher classifies similar judgments into the same group and analyzes the impact of a broader line, a similar line, or a narrower line by studying the performance of each. The specific questions will now be discussed, dealing first with the questions designed to measure posture and second with those designed to measure the marketing mix.

The degree of innovation offered by the entrant was assessed by executives, from the viewpoint of customers, relative to the offerings of incumbents, on a three-point scale: major innovation, incremental innovation, and similar offering. a major innovation was defined as a product or service for customer needs that had *never* been served before. An incremental innovation was defined as a product or service attempting to serve customer needs already being served by existing products but with a new technology or method. A similar offering was defined as a product or service attempting to serve customer needs already being served by existing businesses with basically the same technology or method. The major innovation degree was not relevant to this study because a business offering such an innovation would be starting a new industry. It was included to act as a check against including industry innovators in the sample as opposed to entrants into a going product-market. Only the latter are included in this study.

Entry scale was calculated from two figures provided by executives. The first is the standard capacity of the business in the first two years of entry, defined as the sales value of the maximum output the business can sustain with (1) facilities normally in operation, (2) the product mix during the first two years of commercialization, and (3) current constraints. The second figure is the estimated size of the total served market in the first two years of entry. Entry scale is standard capacity divided by market size and is a continuous variable.

Vertical integration of the entrant was assessed by its executives, relative to incumbents, on a 3-point scale: more than leading competitors, about the same, or less than leading competitors. These judgments were made for both backward and forward integration.

Turning to the marketing mix elements, price was judged by asking executives to estimate their average level of selling prices relative to the average price of leading competitors. Competitors' average price was set at 1.00 and, for example, a price about 5 percent higher than competitors was reported as 1.05.

Product quality was estimated by asking executives to judge the percentage of their sales volume accounted for by products and services that were "superior," "equivalent," and "inferior" to those of leading competitors. The relative product quality percentage used in the analysis is the difference between the superior quality and inferior quality percentages.

Measuring breadth of product line has already been explained in the opening paragraph. Market segmentation within the served market was measured on three bases: type of customers, number of customers, and size of customers. Executives were asked to estimate the breadth of segment served by their business, relative to the average breadth of its leading competitors.

Managers were asked about two aspects of channel decisions. First, they were asked to provide a yes/no answer to the question whether they introduced new channels of distribution. Second, they were asked to compare on a 3-point scale their coverage of immediate customers relative to incumbents.

Improved service was measured by asking for a relative comparison of the quality of services provided to end users in conjunction with the sale of products and services. Relative absolute dollar expenditures on the sales force, advertising, and sales promotion were also measured in this way.

These questions number fifteen, of which four refer to posture—degree of product integration, relative backward integration, relative forward integration, and entry scale— and the remaining eleven refer to the marketing mix. Responses to three of the questions form continuous variables—entry scale, relative price, and relative product quality—while responses to the other twelve form discrete variables on 3-point or 5-point scales. The intervals on the discrete variables are assumed to form difference-scale variables.

IDENTIFYING ENTRY STRATEGY

Table 41 shows the distribution of the sample on the elements of strategic posture. About two-thirds of the sample entered with an incremental innovation; that is, they attempted to serve customer needs with a method or technology that differed from that offered by incumbents. The sample was more evenly spread among the three measures of relative backward integration. In contrast, almost four-fifths of the sample claimed to have entered with about the same degree of relative forward integration as the incumbents

Slightly more than half the sample, twenty-one entrants, chose a production entry scale that amounted to more than

TABLE 41. DISTRIBUTION OF THE SAMPLE ON ENTRY
STRATEGY POSTURE

Product or Service Innovation at Time of Entry	Number	Percent		
Incremental innovation	26	65		
Similar offering	14	35		
	40	100		

Relative Integration in First Two Years	Backward		Forward	
	Number	Percent	Number	Percent
Less than competitors	10	25	3	8
About the same	17	43	31	77
More than competitors	13	32	6	15
	40	100	40	100

Entry Scale = Standard Capacity ÷ Market Size, First Two Years	Number	Percent
Less than 10%	12	31
10–19%	7	18
20–29%	4	10
30–39%	1	3
40–49%	4	10
50–59%	2	5
90% +	9	23
(max. 3,353%)	39[a]	100

Median = 22%

[a] One missing value.

20 percent share of the total served market size in the first two years. The median entry scale was a capacity capable of producing 22 percent of the total market in the first two years; the range was 1 percent to 3,353 percent. Evidently, half these entrants planned to be major factors in their entered product-markets, at least according to the size of market in the first two years. However, the rapid total market growth rates noted in chapter 8 reduced these production entry scales over time. For example, if the total market grows at 50 percent per year—a not uncommon situation in this sample—an entrant with a production entry scale of 25 percent in the first two years, with no further

capacity additions, has a production scale of 17 percent in the third year and 11 percent in the fourth year.

Although regarded as a strategic variable and therefore partially under management control, entry scale is also affected by product-market economies of scale and investment indivisibility. Where these factors are significant, management has little control over the scale variable. In this connection, it is relevant to note that of the nine entrants with an entry scale above 90 percent, two entered process industries (where indivisibilities of investment are more frequent), four entered components industries, and three refused to supply their SIC number. It is unfortunate that incomplete data prevent fuller analysis of production entry scales.

Table 42 shows the distribution of the sample in the first two years on the price, quality, length of line, market segment served, distribution, and customer services elements of the marketing mix. Ten out of forty entrants were price cutters; almost the same number, nine entrants, matched incumbents' prices, while the remaining twenty-one entrants entered with a higher price than the incumbent businesses. Most entrants judged their product quality to be higher than the incumbents'; twenty-eight claimed superior quality, five matched incumbents' quality, and seven reported inferior product quality. It is interesting to note that the mean product quality percentage recorded by 454 established businesses in the PIMS data base for 1970–1973 was 24 percent. The mean for this sample of entrant businesses was 39 percent and the median was even higher at 50 percent. It is clear from this comparison that, on average, managers of entrant businesses believed that they offered a very high level of product quality.[1]

It is also apparent from table 42 that most of the entrants offered a less broad product line and served a narrower market segment than incumbent businesses. About 50 percent of the sample reported a less broad product line and

---

1. Data on relative price, quality, and services collected for the second two years of entry indicate that most entrants showed no major change from their opening position over that time.

TABLE 42. DISTRIBUTION OF THE SAMPLE ON ELEMENTS OF
THE MARKETING MIX, FIRST TWO YEARS

Relative Price (1.00 = Same as Competitors)	Number	Percent	Relative Quality (% Superior − % Inferior)	Number	Percent
Less than 1.00	10	25	Less than 0%	7	18
1.00	9	23	0%	5	12
1.01–1.05	7	18	17.5–39%	6	15
1.06–1.10	3	7	40–69%	8	20
1.11–1.15	3	7	70–99%	6	15
1.16–5.00	8	20	100%	8	20
	40	100		40	100
Mean	1.27		Mean	39%	
(Standard deviation)	(0.87)		(Standard deviation)	(50)	
Median	1.02		Median	50%	

Length of Product Line	Number	Percent
Less broad	24	60
Same breadth	7	18
Broader	9	22
	40	100

Market Segment	Types of Customers		Number of Customers		Size of Customers	
	Number	Percent	Number	Percent	Number	Percent
Less than competitors	16	40	24	60	1	3
About the same	19	48	9	22	30	75
More than competitors	5	12	7	18	9	22
	40	100	40	100	40	100

Distribution	Number	Percent
Followed existing channels	31	79
Introduced new channels	8	21
	39[a]	100
Greater number of immediate customers	4	10
About the same number of immediate customers	16	41
Fewer immediate customers	19	49
	39[a]	100

Quality of Customer Services	Number	Percent
Worse than incumbents	4	10
About the same	15	38
Better than incumbents	21	52
	40	100

[a] One missing value.

another 18 percent reported a line of similar breadth. A similar distribution occurred on the number of customers served: 60 percent served fewer and 22 percent served about the same number as incumbents. Entrants also showed a tendency to serve fewer types of customers than the incumbent businesses. Only on the third aspect of market segmentation, size of customers, did entrants match incumbents' existing market: 75 percent of the sample reported that they served customers of about the same size as those served by incumbents.

This sample of entrants contained very few distribution innovators: only eight, or 21 percent, introduced new channels of distribution. Conversely, the improved customer service strategy was used much more extensively: at least half the sample, twenty-one entrants, offered a better quality of customer services; only four entrants reported a worse level of customer services.

The sample distribution on these elements of the mix suggests that, in comparison with the incumbents, most entrants adopted a marketing mix of:

- less broad market segment
- higher prices and higher quality
- narrower product line
- superior services
- similar distribution channels

This mix represents a modest marketing strategy: higher prices, narrower segments, and narrower product lines, in particular, should theoretically limit the share that entrants could achieve. A mix with low potential market share would seem to conflict with the large production entry scales shown in table 41. It is possible, however, that in their production scale decision, entrant managers were allowing for total market growth or that they faced indivisibilities of investment. It is also possible that the apparent mismatch between production and market scale represented a major strategic mistake committed by this sample on average. To make an obvious point—economies of production scale are only realized if the output is sold to customers on a sustained basis.

An entry mix with low potential market share was more

consistent with entrants' decisions on their relative absolute dollar marketing expenditures. At least half the entrants reported that they spent less than incumbents on sales force, advertising, and promotion expenditures (table 43). A third of the sample reported that they outspent incumbents on sales force expenditures, while only eight, or one-fifth, outspent incumbents on advertising and promotion.[2]

Types of Mix

Of course, just looking at the total sample distribution is not a sufficient means of identifying types of mix. Much as was done in chapter 7 when identifying types of relatedness, the correlation matrix among these elements and the responses of individual businesses were examined to see whether similar values on different elements occurred together.

Table 44 shows the correlation matrix of the elements of posture and mix described above. It is immediately apparent that the coefficients are, in general, higher than those shown in table 24 in chapter 7 for the degree of association among questions measuring relatedness. It appears that there is more overlap among entry strategy elements than among aspects of relatedness, as would be expected given that strategies should be internally consistent (see any basic text, for example, Buzzell et al. 1972: 329–331).

It is helpful to organize this discussion around three kinds of associations: those between pairs of posture aspects; those between posture and mix; and those between pairs of marketing mix elements.

In general, correlation between pairs of posture aspects is low.[3]

---

2. As with relative price, quality, and services, most entrants showed no major change in their opening position on relative marketing expenditures during the second two years.

3. Because this matrix involves both continuous and discrete variables, and tests of significance are subject to the caveats noted in chapter 7. With this cautionary note in mind, a correlation coefficient of 0.43 or higher is statistically significantly different from zero at a level of 0.01 (35 degrees of freedom), while a coefficient of 0.34 or higher is significant at 0.03.

TABLE 43. DISTRIBUTION OF THE SAMPLE ON RELATIVE ABSOLUTE DOLLAR MARKETING
EXPENDITURES, FIRST TWO YEARS

	Sales Force		Advertising		Promotion	
	Number	*Percent*	*Number*	*Percent*	*Number*	*Percent*
Spent less than incumbents	21	52	21	52	24	60
Spent about the same	6	15	11	28	8	20
Spent more than incumbents	13	33	8	20	8	20
	40	100	40	100	40	100

Correlation coefficients are somewhat higher between posture and mix. The correlation between degree of product innovation and relative quality is -0.36, indicating that managers of entrants with an incremental innovation judged their product quality to be higher than did managers of entrants with a similar offering. Similarly, correlation between product innovation and relative services at -0.45 and relative promotion expenditures at -0.41 indicates that managers of entrants with an incremental innovation thought they offered relatively more after-sales services and promotion than their competitors.

Correlation between entry scale and elements of the marketing mix is significant for relative quality (0.39), breadth of customer numbers (0.36), and relative expenditures on the sales force (0.36), advertising (0.35), and promotion (0.52). These correlations indicate a tendency for production scale and market scale to complement each other. Bearing in mind the low capacity utilization noted earlier, it seems likely that the degree of complementarity between these two aspects was not high enough.

Finally, associations between pairs of the marketing mix should be noted. These can be divided into two categories: those among elements that might be expected to be measuring a similar element of the mix and those pointing to different types of marketing mix. An obvious example of the first kind is the three elements of market segment: the type, number, and size of end customers served. Type and number of customers have high correlation at 0.64, but the correlation between these two and size of customers is low. It seems likely that type and number are measuring a similar aspect of market segmentation and one could be dropped, or the two combined, in further analysis to save degrees of freedom.

Another example can be seen among the three elements of relative marketing expenditures: sales force, advertising, and promotion. The extent to which these elements of the mix are substitutes and complements is one of the finer, more intangible, aspects of marketing strategy. The coefficients here are 0.46 between relative sales force and advertising expenditures, 0.51 between the former and promotion expenditures, and 0.65 between relative adver-

TABLE 44. CORRELATION MATRIX OF 16 ASPECTS OF ENTRY STRATEGY, FIRST TWO YEARS ($n = 35$)[a]

	Posture						Marketing Mix	
	Product Innovation	Vertical Integration Backward	Vertical Integration Forward	Entry Scale	Relative Price	Relative Quality	Product Line Length	Breadth of Customer Types
Product Innovation	1.00							
Vertical Integration Backward	0.18	1.00						
Vertical Integration Forward	-0.09	0.23	1.00					
Entry Scale	-0.26	0.31	0.19	1.00				
Relative Price	-0.13	-0.13	0.14	-0.16	1.00			
Relative Quality	-0.36	0.22	0.29	0.39	0.20	1.00		
Product Line Length	-0.29	0.04	0.44	0.23	0.18	0.16	1.00	
Breadth of Customer Types	-0.22	0.09	0.48	0.15	0.25	0.40	0.39	1.00
Breadth of Customer Numbers	-0.25	0.15	0.70	0.36	0.10	0.31	0.59	0.64
Breadth of Customer Size	-0.15	0.30	0.07	0.12	0.12	0.17	0.31	0.15
Distribution Channels	-0.39	-0.04	0.36	0.05	-0.14	0.33	0.21	0.13
Distribution Coverage	0.19	0.01	-0.29	-0.26	0.04	-0.03	-0.21	-0.05
Relative Services	-0.45	-0.03	0.34	0.27	0.37	0.31	0.21	0.14
Relative Sales Force Expenditures	-0.21	0.31	0.09	0.36	-0.30	0.41	0.03	-0.13
Relative Advertising Expenditures	-0.18	0.13	0.46	0.35	-0.22	0.46	0.20	0.25
Relative Promotion Expenditures	-0.41	0.23	0.43	0.52	-0.26	0.43	0.27	0.27

Marketing Mix (Continued)

	Breadth of Customer Numbers	Breadth of Customer Size	Distribution Channels	Distribution Coverage	Relative Services	Relative Sales Force Expenditures	Relative Advertising Expenditures	Relative Promotion Expenditures
Breadth of Customer Numbers	1.00							
Breadth of Customer Size	0.12	1.00						
Distribution Channels	0.43	-0.01	1.00					
Distribution Coverage	-0.48	-0.09	-0.28	1.00				
Relative Services	0.24	0.16	0.29	-0.06	1.00			
Relative Sales Force Expenditures	0.09	0.16	0.20	0.13	0.19	1.00		
Relative Advertising Expenditures	0.52	-0.09	0.38	-0.20	0.42	0.46	1.00	
Relative Promotion Expenditures	0.47	0.12	0.44	-0.36	0.40	0.51	0.62	1.00

[a] Missing values excluded.

tising and promotion expenditures. The magnitude and positive signs of these coefficients indicate that the three elements tend to be complementary, at least in the judgment of the respondents, and they could be combined into one variable.

Turning to associations pointing to different types of mix, there is a positive association between relative product quality and breadth of customer types served (0.40), as well as between quality and relative expenditures on sales force (0.41), advertising (0.46), and promotion (0.43). These correlations suggest that high values on these elements tend to be grouped together and could represent an aggressive mix, whereas low values could represent a modest mix.

Product line length is positively associated with breadth of customer types (0.39) and numbers (0.59) served. These associations suggest another mix based on breadth—a fuller product line aimed at a greater variety and larger number of customers.

A surprising finding (in table 44) is that relative price has low correlation with all the other elements. There is no immediate explanation for this observation and further analysis is needed.

In the search for different types of entry strategy, factor analysis of the elements of market posture and the elements of the marketing mix naturally suggests itself. Factor analysis is an aid to the identification of a more fundamental structure or theme that explains the observed interdependencies among the sixteen elements shown in table 44. Factor analysis was used on these data but, before presenting the results, two theoretical points and one research strategy point should be noted. First, factor analysis assumes that the variables are multivariate normally distributed, but discrete variables do not meet this assumption. Second, factor analysis is a linear combination of variables and it is not reasonable to believe that the true relationship among all these variables is linear. In view of these points, factor analysis was applied to these data in the spirit of searching for managerially useful insights while bearing in mind theoretical caveats.

The point of research strategy centers on the low correlations observed in table 44 between two elements of posture and twelve marketing mix elements. This finding is a rebuttal of the reasoning in chapter 2 that posture and mix decisions should be related. Clearly, other variables influence the composition of the marketing mix to a greater extent. In view of this finding, it was decided to search for different types of marketing mixes and present two analyses of the impact of entry strategy on performance—one dealing with the elements of posture and one dealing with different types of marketing mixes. This strategem also has the advantage of revealing the influence of elements such as the degree of innovation and of integration which have independent interest to managers.

Table 45 shows the outcome of the extraction of three factors from the twelve elements of the marketing mix by the principal components method. These three factors were derived from varimax rotation which enhances the variance among the factors and, therefore, their interpretability. The rotation was applied to normalized variables

TABLE 45. TWELVE MARKETING MIX ELEMENTS REDUCED TO THREE PRINCIPAL COMPONENTS, VARIMAX ROTATED, AND NORMALIZED, FIRST TWO YEARS

	Loadings		
Marketing Mix Element Relative to Incumbents	*Factor 1 Aggressiveness*	*Factor 2 Breadth*	*Factor 3 Luxuriousness*
Price	−0.36	−0.01	0.74
Product quality	0.54	0.10	0.50
Breadth of product line	0.06	0.49	0.31
Breadth of customer types	0.06	0.52	0.46
Breadth of customer numbers	0.27	0.86	0.21
Breadth of customer size	0.13	0.07	0.35
Distribution channels	0.42	0.28	0.06
Distribution coverage	−0.10	−0.61	0.10
Customer services	0.38	0.15	0.50
Sales force expenditures	0.79	−0.19	0.03
Advertising expenditures	0.72	0.30	0.09
Promotion expenditures	0.75	0.40	0.04
Sum of Loadings Squared	*2.54*	*2.04*	*1.54*

Total sum of loadings squared = 6.12
Number of variables = 12
Explanation of observed variance = 6.12/12 = 51%

so that the derived factors would depend equally on the twelve marketing mix elements.

As a result of the factor analysis, entrants' relative price now appears prominently. Price has a negative influence on factor 1 with a loading of −0.36 and a highly positive influence on factor 3 with a loading of 0.74. The negative influence of price on factor 1 is combined with positive influences from entrants' relative product quality (loading 0.54) and opening new channels of distribution (0.42), and highly positive influences from entrants' relative expenditures on their sales force (0.79), advertising (0.72), and promotion (0.72). Because lower prices, higher quality, and greater marketing expenditures amount to a very aggressive marketing mix, factor 1 has been called "aggressiveness."

Factor 2 is heavily loaded on the number of customers served (0.86), the coverage of immediate customers (−0.61), the breadth of customer types served (0.52), and the breadth of the product line (0.49). Because this factor concentrates more on the dimensions of the market segment served by the entrant, it has been labeled "breadth."

Factor 3 is the opposite of factor 1 on price, showing a positive influence, but similar in that product quality has a high and positive loading of 0.50. Customer services also has a high positive loading of 0.50 on factor 3. Because higher prices, better quality, and improved customer services suggest a premium pricing approach to a premium product-service combination, factor 3 has been called "luxuriousness."

These three factors explain 51 percent of the observed variance of the twelve elements of the marketing: factor 1 explains 21 percent, factor 2 explains 17 percent, and factor 3 explains 13 percent. Naturally, the question arises as to the significance of this factor analysis. Zaltman and Burger (1975: 509) have suggested the following as criteria of factor analysis significance:

- Each beginning ratio of the squared sum of variable loadings on a factor to the total number of variables is greater than 1.
- The loadings of the factors after varimax rotation are larger than 0.3.

• The variance explained of all factors in the factor analysis is greater than 40 percent.
• No variable loads significantly on more than one factor.

The factor analysis performed here rates satisfactory on the first three of these criteria, but fails to meet the fourth. Defining significant loading at 0.35 or more, price, quality, and customer services load significantly on factors 1 and 3, promotion expenditures on factors 1 and 2, and breadth of customer types on factors 2 and 3. A four factor extraction was tried but it did not improve performance on the fourth criterion, besides failing to meet the first; furthermore, the total explained variance increased only 6 percentage points to 57 percent, which is a small gain compared with the increase in the number of factors and loss of 1 degree of freedom.

In managerial terms, this three-factor analysis does provide some useful insight into the types of marketing mix used by this sample. For example, managers of a prospective entrant with an incremental innovation often have to choose between a skim or penetration price, without having to lower the quality of their product. Factor 1 presumably captures the penetration pricing decision, combined with heavier marketing expenditures; whereas factor 3 captures the skim price decision, combined with superior services to the customer. Factor 2 addresses another important entry mix decision: the breadth of market to be served. It will, therefore, be of managerial interest to analyze performance by these three factors.

Five Price-Quality Combinations

At the same time, it is clear that managers of entrants must also choose explicitly among different price-quality combinations. For example, an average product quality can be combined with a lower price. It also seems of value, therefore, to identify the price-quality combinations used by these entrants and analyze their impact on performance as a separate dimension. Based on inspection of individual responses and building on the mix types developed in chapter 2, three price strategies and three quality strategies were identified and then combined into five price-quality combinations. The three price strategies were: price cutters (a relative price 0.95 or less); similar price (a relative price ranging from 0.98 to 1.04); and high price (a relative price 1.05 and higher). The three product quality groupings were: inferior quality (negative relative quality); better or similar quality (relative quality ranging from 0 to 55 percent at the midpoint of positive quality rankings); and high quality (relative quality higher than 55 percent).

In grouping these strategies to form price-quality combinations, it was noticed first that all the nine price cutters but one had high or better/similar quality. It was decided to group these eight together into one price-quality combination called "price cutters and high/similar quality." Nine entrants used both high prices and high quality and these formed another combination, called, obviously, "high prices and high quality." Of the other eight entrants in the high price group, six offered better/similar quality and these formed another price-quality combination, labeled "high prices and better/similar quality."

Of the twelve entrants offering similar prices, eight offered better/similar quality: these formed another price-quality combination called "similar prices and better/similar quality."

The seven entrants left over from this classification offered inferior quality at varying relative price levels. It was decided to put these in a separate group, called "inferior quality/assorted prices." The five price-quality combinations are shown in table 46.

This section so far has identified four elements of market posture, derived three more fundamental factors from the twelve marketing mix variables and identified five price-quality combinations. These different characteristics of entry strategy were analyzed for their impact on performance and the results are presented in the next section.

DEGREE OF PRODUCT INNOVATION

Entrants with an incremental innovation face the tasks of developing the manufacturing processes for their prod-

TABLE 46. FIVE PRICE-QUALITY ENTRY STRATEGY
COMBINATIONS, FIRST TWO YEARS

Combinations	Subsample Size	Relative Price		Relative Quality Percentage	
		Mean	Median	Mean	Median
High price and high quality	9	2.03	1.09	81	80
High price and better/similar quality	6	1.40	1.24	29	33
Similar price and better/similar quality	8	1.01	1.00	28	20
Price cutters and high/similar quality	8	0.88	0.88	69	78
Inferior quality/assorted prices	7	1.01	1.00	−40	−20

uct and attaining an acceptable level of product performance. In contrast, entrants with a similar offering can learn
from existing processes or, even better, buy fully developed equipment and inputs from experienced suppliers.
These considerations should result in higher manufactur-
ing/sales and R&D/sales ratios for entrants with incremental innovations.

The marketing task faced by these two types of entrant
is different in kind but probably similar in its cost as a
ratio to sales revenues. Entrants with an incremental innovation must persuade customers to switch to their new
method or technology of solving problems, which involves
some customer risk. Most will be reluctant to adopt the
entrants' product or service without extensive trial and
technical sales service. Therefore, these entrants face a
costly market development task at a time when sales revenues are low and a high ratio of marketing expenses to
sales is likely to result.

Conversely, entrants with a similar offering do not have
to sell a new method but do have to assure customers that
there is an advantage in breaking their relationships, probably long-established, with their existing suppliers. This
can be termed a market penetration task and could involve
costs such that their ratio to sales is just as high as for the
market development task.

TABLE 47. OPERATING AND CAPITAL STRUCTURE RATIOS BY DEGREE OF PRODUCT INNOVATION, FIRST FOUR YEARS

		Years 1 and 2		Years 3 and 4	
Percentage Operating Ratios		*Incremental Innovation* (n = 26)	*Similar Offering* (n = 14)	*Incremental Innovation* (n = 18)	*Similar Offering* (n = 10)
Purchasing/sales	Mean	47	47	46	47
	Median	46	39	44	44
Manufacturing/sales	Mean	41	36	29	26
	Median	34	27	31	23
R&D/sales	Mean	66	22 (0.01 probability)	31	8 (0.05 probability)
	Median	36	10	12	5
Marketing/sales	Mean	40	42	26	24
	Median	35	32	20	31
Percentage Capital Structure Ratios					
Receivables/sales	Mean	18	16	19	16
	Median	15	17	13	15
Inventory/sales[a,b]	Mean	41	29	64	24
	Median	27	25	24	25
Investment/sales	Mean	264	130 (0.14 probability)	258	96 (0.16 probability)
	Median	106	98	80	60

[a] Service business excluded from Incremental Innovation and two from Similar Offering in both time periods.
[b] Two missing values from Incremental Innovation.

Data in table 48 suggest that the financial performance of entrants with a similar offering is somewhat better than incremental innovators in the first two years. For example, mean return on sales is −113 percent for incremental innovators, against −58 percent for entrants with a similar offering. This financial performance is surprising in view of the lower relative share for incremental innovators. Relative share at 62 percent for incremental innovators is some 49 points higher than the 13 percent recorded by similar offering entrants in the first two years. Median relative share at 25 percent is about double the 12 percent median for similar offering entrants. The resolution, at least partially, of inferior financial performance from higher share appears to be the much higher R&D/sales ratio of the incremental innovators. Table 48 shows that mean R&D/sales at 66 percent for incremental innovators is significantly higher than the 22 percent shown by entrants with a similar offering. Results are similar in the second two years: only R&D/sales shows a difference that is significant at commonly accepted levels.

In the second two years, financial performance of similar offering entrants continued to be somewhat better than incremental innovators. However, similar offering entrants could not match the relative market share of incremental innovators. Given the benefits of share, this finding suggests that the incremental innovators were building a better business for the long-run than the similar offering entrants. We can speculate that these data are saying to us that it takes longer to establish a new business based on an incremental offering but that the financial performance of such a business over its entire life will be superior to a similar offering entrant. If validated in subsequent research, the executive implication is the need for more patience with an incremental innovator business.

RELATIVE VERTICAL INTEGRATION

Vertical integration of inputs or distributive systems by incumbents is often listed as a barrier to entry. If the entrant decides to match incumbents' degree of vertical

TABLE 48. PERFORMANCE MEASURES BY DEGREE OF PRODUCT INNOVATION, FIRST FOUR YEARS

Percentage Performance Measures	Years 1 and 2			Years 3 and 4		
	Incremental Innovation (n = 26)	Similar Offering (n = 14)	Probability <0.2 and R²	Incremental Innovation (n = 18)	Similar Offering (n = 10)	Probability above 0.2 Not Shown
Cash flow						
Mean	−113	−83		−53	−37	
Median	−83	−71	(R² = 0.06)	−33	−35	
(R² = 0.02)						
Return on investment						
Mean	−96	−43	(Probability 0.04)	−56	−27	0.2
Median	−42	−38	(R² = 0.05)	−14	−7	
(R² = 0.02)						
Return on sales						
Mean	−113	−58	(Probability 0.04)	−49	−15	.14
Median	−73	−31	(R² = 0.05)	−17	−3	
(R² = 0.03)						
Relative share						
Mean	62	13	(Probability 0.002)	73	9	0.01
Median	25	12	(R² = 0.16)	16	6	
(R² = 0.15)						

integration, capital costs of the entry are higher. Alternatively, if the entrants decide to enter at a lower degree of integration, the production cost curve may well lie above that of the incumbents. This familiar reasoning leads to the proposition that in this sample of actual entrants, those who report relatively more integration should have lower operating costs than those who entered in a less integrated posture. Lower costs are likely to lead to better financial performance, although achieving this also depends on the amount of investment behind the entry.

However, there appears to be little difference in financial performance among three degrees of relative backward integration (see table 49). There does appear to be a difference in relative market share performance with the median at 7 percent for less backward integrated entrants and 25 percent for more backward integrated entrants. Data for the second two years show a similar picture of little difference in financial performance and higher relative share for more backward integrated entrants. All that can safely be said from this table is that we need more data to understand the impact of relative backward integration on performance. The R^2 are the lowest yet seen in the study.

The data on relative forward integration are a little more interpretable but extreme caution is necessary in drawing conclusions because cell sample sizes are small. Table 50 shows that mean and median financial performance tended to improve as entrants' posture on degree of relative forward integration increased. For example, median ROI is −56 percent for "less," −41 percent for "same," and −17 percent for "more" forward integration. Trends in the second two years were not analyzed because of even smaller cell sizes.

One reason why more forward integrated entrants show better financial performance is that they obtain higher relative market share. Analysis of their operating ratios shows that these entrants also have lower marketing/sales and R&D/sales ratios. In the first two years, median marketing/sales is 37 percent, 45 percent, and 19 percent for "less," "same," and "more" forward integration, respectively. Average R&D/sales ratio is 53 percent, 54 percent,

TABLE 49. PERFORMANCE MEASURES BY RELATIVE BACKWARD INTEGRATION, FIRST FOUR YEARS

		Relative Backward Integration							
Percentage Performance Measures		Years 1 and 2			Probability <0.2 and R^2	Years 3 and 4			Probability above 0.2 Not Shown
		Less (n = 10)	Same (n = 17)	More (n = 13)		Less (n = 9)	Same (n = 13)	More (n = 6)	
Cash flow/investment ($R^2 = 0.01$)	Mean	-93	-113	-96		-39	-53	-48	
	Median	-71	-84	-76	($R^2 = 0.02$)	-23	-34	-34	
Return on investment ($R^2 = 0.01$)	Mean	-53	-100	-68	(Less vs. Same = 0.13)	-32	-55	-41	
	Median	-41	-39	-45	($R^2 = 0.03$)	-14	-7	-23	
Return on sales ($R^2 = 0.08$)	Mean	-87	-92	-101	($R^2 = 0$)	-80	-21	-18	Less vs. More = 0.16
	Median	-70	-34	-79		-17	-3	-21	
Relative share[a] ($R^2 = 0.09$)	Mean	29	51	46	($R^2 = 0.02$)	14	62	66	(Less vs. More = 0.07)
	Median	7	17	25		3	12	14	

[a] One missing value excluded from less, same, and more in second two years.

TABLE 50. PERFORMANCE MEASURES BY RELATIVE FORWARD INTEGRATION, FIRST TWO YEARS

| Percentage Performance Measures | | Relative Forward Integration, Years 1 and 2 | | | |
		Less (n = 3)	Same (n = 31)	More (n = 6)	Probability above 0.2 Not Shown
Cash flow/investment	Mean	-90	-111	-65	Less vs. More = .019
($R^2 = 0.09$)	Median	-84	-88	-66	Same vs. More = 0.002
Return on investment	Mean	-40	-93	-20	Same vs. More = 0.01
($R^2 = 0.07$)	Median	-56	-41	-17	Less vs. Same = 0.09
Return on sales	Mean	-103	-103	-41	
($R^2 = 0.03$)	Median	-71	-44	-41	
Relative share[a]	Mean	9	34	107	Less vs. More = 0.01
($R^2 = 0.23$)					Same vs. More = 0.02
	Median	10	11	87	Less vs. Same = 0.05

[a] Missing values from Same in first two years.

and 33 percent for the same three groups. It seems, therefore, that being more forward integrated than incumbents is associated with higher share and lower marketing and R&D ratios than being less forward integrated. This finding is in accord with propositions about the benefits of integration. On the other hand, more relative backward integration did not seem to bestow these benefits.

ENTRY SCALE

Hypotheses about the likely impact of entry production scale on performance cannot be made with an absolute measure; also needed is the minimum efficient scale applicable to each particular product-market entered. Lacking these data, all that can be suggested here is that larger entry production scale, up to a point, is likely to improve performance provided it is matched with a larger entry market scale and provided that larger scale entrants achieve high market share (which, as noted in chapter 6, helps financial performance).

Medium entry production scale is associated with the best financial performance in both the first and second two years of entry (see table 51). For example, medium scale entrants reported median ROI of 26 percent, compared with −86 percent for small scale entrants and −39 percent for large scale entrants. The explanation for this finding seems to be that larger production scale usually also meant higher relative market share (correlation between the two is 0.64), except for six large production scale entrants who achieved a relative share of less than 10 percent. These six entrants experienced poor financial performance and caused the performance of the large scale group to drop below that of the medium scale group. Thus, larger entry production scale has a favorable impact on financial performance to the extent that it is combined with higher relative market share. This linkage reinforces the point made earlier that production economies from building the appropriate size plant will only be realized if the minimum optimum level of volume is actually sold to customers on a sustained basis.

TABLE 51. PERFORMANCE MEASURES BY ENTRY PRODUCTION SCALE, FIRST FOUR YEARS

| | | Entry Production Scale | | | | | | | |
| | | Years 1 and 2 (n = 39) | | | | Years 3 and 4 (n = 27) | | | |
Percentage Performance Measures		*Small (10% and Less) (n = 12)*	*Medium (11–30%) (n = 12)*	*Large (40% or More) (n = 15)*	*Probability < 0.2 and R²*	*Small (6% and Less) (n = 9)*	*Medium (7–36%) (n = 8)*	*Large (47% or More) (n = 10)*	*Probability < 0.2 and R²*
Cash flow/ investment	Mean	-120	-88	-103	Same vs. More = 0.11	-41	-32	-66	
(R² = 0.06)	Median	-96	-74	-78		-32	-20	-34	(R² = 0.06)
Return on investment	Mean	-104	-58	-78	Same vs. More = 0.19	-29	-30	-76	Same vs. Less = 0.20
(R² = 0.04)	Median	-86	-26	-39		-16	-5	-6	(R² = 0.05)
Return on sales	Mean	-152	-38	-99	Same vs. More = 0.02 / More vs. Less = 0.04 / Same vs. Less = 0.08	-68	-14	-29	Same vs. More = 0.18
(R² = 0.15)	Median	-96	-29	-79		-22	-3	-5	(R² = 0.06)
Relative share[a]	Mean	2	46	82	Same vs. More = 0.01 / Same vs. Less = 0.001 / More vs. Less = 0.10	5	20	138	Same vs. Less = 0.002 / Same vs. More = 0.05 / More vs. Less = 0.009
	Median	1	23	68		3	12	92	(R² = 0.52)

[a] One missing value from Medium and two from High in first two years.

PERFORMANCE AND ENTRY STRATEGY: MARKETING MIX FACTORS

It is possible to make common-sense conjectures about the impact of the three factors of aggressiveness, breadth, and luxuriousness. Aggressive entrants, representing relatively lower prices, better quality, and higher marketing expenditures, should obtain higher relative market share but poorer financial performance in the first two years than entrants with a less aggressive mix. Financial performance should improve in the second two years as the benefits from the higher share begin to take effect. Table 52 shows data that suggest that aggressive entrants did record better financial performance in the first two years than those with medium or low aggressiveness. With the exception of the return on sales measure, however, the differences on the means are not statistically significant. Aggressive entrants did show considerably better relative share performance with a median relative share at 80 percent, compared with 15 percent and 2 percent for medium and low aggressiveness, respectively. Again, the R^2 on relative share was the highest at 0.29; this finding recurs time and again: the concepts in the analytical framework seem to be able to explain relative share variation to a most satisfactory degree.

In the second two years, the mean and median differences were more marked and there is a stronger suggestion that aggressive entrants had better financial performance. For example, ROI mean was −8 percent, median 3 percent, for aggressive entrants; −100 percent, median −17 percent, for medium aggressiveness; and −26 percent, median −4 percent, for low aggressiveness. Their stronger financial performance in the second two years probably stems from their superior relative share in the first two years.

Entrants with a broader mix, representing broader product lines and broader types and numbers of customers than incumbents, could also be expected to have poor financial performance but the highest relative share in the first two years. The breadth of their segment and line gives them the potential for higher relative share but the costs of

TABLE 52. PERFORMANCE MEASURES BY FACTOR 1: AGGRESSIVENESS, FIRST FOUR YEARS

Percentage Performance Measures		Years 1 and 2				Years 3 and 4			
		Low (n = 13)	Medium (n = 13)	High (n = 12)	Probability <0.2 and R²	Low (n = 9)	Medium (n = 9)	High (n = 9)	Probability <0.2 and R²
Cash flow/ investment	Mean	-104	-109	-85		-35	-72	-33	Medium vs. High = 0.12 Low vs. Medium = 0.15
	Median	-83	-90	-74	(R² = 0.07)	-19	-29	-34	(R² = 0.10)
Return on investment	Mean	-78	-94	-45	Medium vs. High = 0.15	-26	-100	-8	Medium vs. High = 0.07 Low vs. Medium = 0.12 Low vs. High = 0.16
	Median	-41	-64	-26	(R² = 0.07)	-4	-17	3	(R² = 0.16)
Return on sales	Mean	-104	-121	-40	Medium vs. High = 0.02 Low vs. High = 0.10	-20	-89	-1	Medium vs. High = 0.07 Low vs. Medium = 0.12 Low vs. High = 0.08
	Median	-52	-96	-32	(R² = 0.10)	-17	-31	3	(R² = 0.16)
Relative share[a]	Mean	19	21	91	Medium vs. High = 0.01 Low vs. High = 0.01	43	9	81	Medium vs. High = 0.01 Low vs. Medium = 0.17
	Median	2	15	80	(R² = 0.29)	11	5	65	(R² = 0.13)

[a] Two missing values from Medium in first and second two years.

implementing this entry mix are likely to be high initially, with financial benefits coming later if the higher share is achieved.

Table 53 indicates the reverse of this expectation on financial performance. Broader entrants showed superior financial performance to moderate breadth entrants. They also appeared to perform better than narrow entrants but the data are less clear. In the second two years, differences among the means and medians were similar but less marked.

In contrast to aggressiveness and breadth, it might be expected that entrants with a high degree of luxuriousness in their entry mix would have superior financial performance but inferior market performance. A luxury mix consists of substantially better relative quality and services, which impact negatively on the income statement, but also of relatively higher prices (the variable with the highest loading on this factor), which should offset the quality and service costs. Higher prices, however, should also limit the size of relative market share achieved by a luxurious mix. Furthermore, the handicaps represented by a lower relative share should impact on financial performance in the second two years. It might be expected, therefore, that luxury mix entrants' financial performance declines over time.

However, table 54 indicates that financial performance according to level of luxuriousness is confused: the means and medians give conflicting signals. Such confusion does not exist on the relative market share measure. In both time periods, on both means and medians, entrants with the most luxurious mix recorded the highest relative market share. This finding is counter to conjecture and no immediate explanation is available.

In summary of the data on the impact of these three factors on performance, breadth is the most discriminating and aggressiveness next, while luxuriousness conveys little information. As for the impact of each factor, it seems that entrants with a broader mix and a more aggressive mix can achieve the best performance on both financial and market measures. It appears that being aggressive and broad enables entrants to obtain a higher relative share,

TABLE 53. PERFORMANCE MEASURES BY FACTOR 2: BREADTH, FIRST FOUR YEARS

Percentage Performance Measures		Years 1 and 2				Years 3 and 4			
		Narrow (n = 12)	Moderate (n = 13)	Broad (n = 13)	Probability <0.2 and R^2	Narrow (n = 9)	Moderate (n = 9)	Broad (n = 9)	Probability <0.2 and R^2
Cash flow/ investment	Mean	-85	-139	-75	Narrow vs. Moderate = 0.02 Moderate vs. Broad = 0.01	-41	-82	-29	Moderate vs. Broad = 0.11 Narrow vs. Moderate = 0.18
	Median	-68	-127	-76	(R^2 = 0.27)	-29	-34	-22	(R^2 = 0.14)
Return on investment	Mean	-51	-132	-34	Narrow vs. Moderate = 0.05 Moderate vs. Broad = 0.02	-26	-95	-22	Moderate vs. Broad = 0.14 Narrow vs. Moderate = 0.16
	Median	-32	-82	-21	(R^2 = 0.19)	-5	-24	-3	(R^2 = 0.11)
Return on sales	Mean	-74	-137	-56	Narrow vs. Moderate = 0.12 Moderate vs. Broad = 0.06	-61	-38	-14	Moderate vs. Broad = 0.14
	Median	-33	-103	-35	(R^2 = 0.10)	-9	-31	-2	(R^2 = 0.05)
Relative share[a]	Mean	36	9	86	Narrow vs. Moderate = 0.09 Moderate vs. Broad = 0.002 Narrow vs. Broad = 0.05	21	7	105	
	Median	4	2	57	(R^2 = 0.26)	7	3	41	(R^2 = 0.30)

[a] Two missing values in each of the three categories in both the first and second two years.

TABLE 54. PERFORMANCE MEASURES BY FACTOR 3: LUXURIOUSNESS, FIRST FOUR YEARS

Percentage Performance Measures		Years 1 and 2				Years 3 and 4			
		Low (n = 12)	Medium (n = 13)	High (n = 13)	Probability <0.2 and R²	Low (n = 9)	Medium (n = 9)	High (n = 9)	Probability <0.2 and R²
Cash flow/ investment	Mean	−77	−119	−102	Low vs. High = 0.04 Low vs. Medium = 0.08	28	−46	−68	Low vs. High = 0.11 Low vs. Medium = 0.19
	Median	−67	−86	−83	(R² = 0.13)	−20	−34	−34	(R² = 0.08)
Return on investment	Mean	−31	−115	−70	Low vs. High = 0.12 Medium vs. High = 0.19 Low vs. Medium = 0.02	−12	−36	−87	Low vs. High = 0.11 Low vs. Medium = 0.13
	Median	−40	−46	−32	(R² = 0.13)	−5	−3	−23	(R² = 0.10)
Return on sales	Mean	−67	−110	−90	Low vs. High = 0.15	−65	−12	−33	Medium vs. High = 0.17 Low vs. Medium = 0.18
	Median	−52	−95	−35	(R² = 0.05)	−8	−2	−17	(R² = 0.05)
Relative share [a]	Mean	9	48	72	Low vs. High = 0.003 Low vs. Medium = 0.05	10	44	92	Low vs. High = 0.04 Low vs. Medium = 0.14 Medium vs. High = 0.18
	Median	8	10	55	(R² = 0.19)	11	10	58	(R² = 0.18)

[a] Three missing values from Medium in first and second two years.

which helps lower their operating ratios and improve their financial performance.

PERFORMANCE AND ENTRY STRATEGY: PRICE-QUALITY COMBINATIONS

Of the five price-quality combinations, the price cutters and high/similar quality group could be expected to exhibit the sharpest contrast on financial and market performance: their relatively lower prices should help them gain share, but lower prices plus higher quality should raise their costs and damge their early financial performance. The two combinations involving high prices could show the best financial performance because their margins may be higher; of these two, however, the high price and high quality combination should show poorer financial performance because of higher costs to deliver their relatively higher quality. Conversely, the two high price combinations should record lower relative shares than the price cutters and high/similar quality combination. The inferior quality and assorted prices combination should show the worst financial and market performance. The performance to be expected from the similar price and better/similar quality is not clear.

The mean and median performance of these five price-quality combinations in the first two years are shown in table 55. Judging by the medians, the price cutters and high/similar quality combination recorded the highest relative share at 57 percent; the next highest were the two high price combinations, with 25 percent and 24 percent respectively. The inferior quality and assorted prices combination recorded the lowest median relative share at 2 percent.

From examination of the medians on the financial measures, it appears that the similar price and better/similar quality combination and the high price and better/similar quality combination recorded the best performance. For example, their median return on sales are 21 percent and 35 percent respectively, whereas the three other combinations show medians of 70 percent or higher. The next

TABLE 55. PERFORMANCE MEASURES BY PRICE-QUALITY COMBINATIONS, FIRST TWO YEARS

Percentage Performance Measures	High Price and High Quality (n = 9)	High Price and Better/Similar Quality (n = 6)	Similar Price and Better/Similar Quality (n = 8)	Price Cutters and High/Similar Quality (n = 8)	Inferior Quality and Assorted Prices (n = 7)
Cash flow/investment (R^2 = 0.12)					
Mean	−120	−79	−83	−123	−90
Median	−110	−76	−66	−87	−71
ROI (R^2 = 0.15)					
Mean	−103	−33	−50	−119	−46
Median	−72	−26	−40	−42	−38
Return on sales (R^2 = 0.05)					
Mean	−128	−65	−80	−85	−79
Median	−73	−21	−35	−87	−70
Relative share (R^2 = 0.19)					
Mean	71	47	16	65	6
Median	25	24	12	57	2

best financial performance appears to come from the inferior quality/assorted prices combination, but any enthusiasm for this finding must be tempered by their low relative share. We may speculate that these entrants achieved their financial results by making a modest entry.

It would seem from median data that a price cutting and high/similar quality combination is best for market position and that higher prices combined with better or similar quality are best for financial performance. Considering that the price cutters offered, on average, a level of product quality as high as the high quality entrants, it seems clear that they offered the best customer bargain. It is probable that they could have lowered their relative quality or raised their prices somewhat without too significant an impact on their share performance and thereby made their financial performance less negative.

Unfortunately, subsample sizes are too small in the second two years of entry to permit useful analysis of subsequent performance. Expectations of performance are not clear, with the possible exception of the price cutters. Their initially higher share should eventually translate into better financial performance.

10. The Impact of Competitive Reaction on Performance

THE FINAL INFLUENCE on entrant performance suggested by the analytical framework in chapter 1 is the type and intensity of the reaction to entry by the incumbent rivals. I also reasoned that reaction is partially triggered by the entrants' strategy and the characteristics of the entered product-market. This chapter is concerned with the impact of reaction on performance and the relationship between reaction and entry strategy and market structure.

In chapter 2, several adjectival typologies of strategy were reviewed. It was decided that the essential features of reaction could be expressed in terms of the elements of the marketing mix. That is, the marketing mix seemed as relevant to incumbents in planning reaction strategy as it did to entrants in planning their entry strategy. The most parsimonious approach, therefore, was to retain the elements of the mix used to analyze entry strategy for analyzing reaction, rather than introducing or refining a typology with yet more terms or concepts. Thus, reaction is studied by identifying changes in prices, productive capacity, products, marketing expenditures, and distribution. In addition, it was also decided to inquire whether incumbents invaded (Knickerbocker 1973) other product-markets of the parent company sponsoring the entrant.

The first task in this chapter is to describe how competitive reaction was measured. The next task is to describe the hypotheses about the nature and intensity of reaction developed from the literature. The final task is to test these hypotheses and assess the performance impact of any observed reaction.

MEASURING COMPETITIVE REACTION

Reaction was defined to have occurred if, after entry, incumbents changed their mix from that immediately[1] prior to entry. Reaction, therefore, like the entry strategy concept, is relative (to what the leading competitors had done before entry) and particularistic (within the context of each product-market entered). It was recognized that incumbents could change their mix for reasons other than the entry of new rivals. In an effort to isolate the reaction due to entry, entrant managers were asked to report reaction that they judged to be a direct response to their arrival in the product-market. Additionally, entrant managers were asked to report these data for the full first two years of entry. It was thought that any reaction beyond two years could come from such a multiplicity of sources that no reliable conclusions could be drawn about the relationship between the entrants' characteristics and reaction.

Three basic types of reaction were envisaged: no change; an increase; and a decrease in an element of the mix. Increases and decreases were broken down into gradations; for example, reaction on price was divided into five gradations of competitive price decreases ranging from "1-5 percent" to "greater than 25 percent."

As a means of summarizing reaction on all five elements measured—price, capacity, product, marketing expenditures, and distribution—an index of reaction was constructed. The maximum level of reaction was assigned 6 points, the next level 4 points, and so on, to no reaction which was assigned 0 points. For example, price decreases greater than 25 percent received 6 points, decreases be-

---

1. It is recognized that some incumbents might have changed their strategy earlier in anticipation of entry or with the objective of forestalling entry. This kind of incumbent reaction was not measured.

tween 11 and 25 percent received 4 points, decreases between 1 and 10 percent received 2 points, and no price changes received no points. The maximum reaction possible under this scheme amounted to 120 points, and the reaction experienced by each business was expressed as a percentage.

COMPETITIVE REACTION HYPOTHESES

Competitive reaction is an important part of both research and decision making in oligopolies because fewness of competitors creates interdependence among rivals' strategies. Unfortunately, the research[2] in this area has met with only limited success. The research problem is that reaction varies according to subjective factors such as competitors' perception of one another, their attitudes to risk, and their interpretation of future market prospects. This problem forced Needham (1969, chap. 7) to conclude: "The exact nature of the reaction . . . cannot be determined by a priori reasoning." This problem is circumvented in oligopoly research by making simple and mechanistic assumptions about potential entrant and incumbent firm conjectures about one another. The result is that the published research to date has limited applicability to the entry decision situation. It does, however, provide a starting point for hypothesis building.

The approach of existing research is to enquire into the ex ante perceptions of entrants about the ex post reactions from incumbents were they to make an entry. The Sylos Postulate (Bain 1956; Sylos 1956; Modigliani 1958) suggests that potential entrants should assume that incumbents will, when entry occurs, maintain output and allow

---

2. The literature is enormous and will not be fully reviewed here. The research commences with Cournot's work, which postulated no reaction to rivals' changes, in duopoly. Stackelberg raised the notion of "leader" and "follower" behavior. More recent approaches include "implicit bargaining" by Fellner and "price leadership" by Markham, both of which assume tacit collusion among rivals. More recently still, game theoretical approaches have been used where a common assumption is that a rival will adopt the reaction that damages its opposite number the most.

price to fall. No particular reasons are given for this assumption except that, from the point of view of a firm planning an entry, it seems safest to assume an unfavorable reaction by the incumbents.

This part of the oligopoly literature also studies how incumbents might influence potential entrants' ex ante perceptions about their ex post reaction, with the objective of limiting entry. For example, Scherer (1971: 226) argues that incumbents can cause potential entrants to believe that the Sylos Postulate is valid by behaving as if they would allow price to fall following entry. In this way, incumbents can adversely influence potential entrants' preentry calculations and, perhaps, prevent entry. Stigler (1966: chap. 12) suggests that a worse reaction than the Sylos Postulate is for the incumbents to increase output. Not only will price fall, but the extra demand is more likely to be supplied by the existing firms rather than the entrant. Thus, incumbents can cause potential entrants to believe that output will be increased upon their entry by investing in capacity additions ahead of the growth of demand (see also, Spence 1974).

Wenders (1971) assumes that incumbents can influence the size of entry scale chosen by the potential entrant and demonstrates mathematically that incumbents' ex post profits are maximized by reducing output. He arrives at this "live and let live" reaction by relating the size of entry to the perceived ex post behavior of incumbents; that is, entry scale can be modulated by the incumbents' behaving as if they would reduce output after entry. In other words, incumbents' preentry behavior signals that small-scale entrants will be accepted into the oligopoly.

One problem with these conclusions is that the models employed exclude the characteristics of the rivals and of the entered market. For example, the Sylos Postulate seems unlikely to hold up in the face of a large entry scale. Such an entrant knows that its output addition to the total market is likely to depress price. Presumably, it has calculated that it can withstand the price drop—perhaps because of parent company cross-subsidization or because initial losses have been capitalized (for purposes of company analysis) in the expectation of long-term gain. But now look at the incumbents. The large-scale entrant is certainly a potential threat to their business. Game theory teaches that the plausibility of a threat varies with the ability of the person making the threat to implement it. Assume that the large-scale entrant is also backed by a parent company that has larger relative size than the parent companies backing the incumbent businesses. Incumbents would probably conclude that the entrant has the ability to mount a campaign to sell its potential output. The potential threat therefore becomes plausible.

What are the incumbents to do? Vernon (1974: chap. 1) argues that strong reaction is unlikely when incumbents are confronted by superior resources. Profit per unit, already cut by the addition of the entrant's output, will be further reduced by a price war (see also, Bhagwati 1970), and there will be little chance of balancing this with increased volume if demand is price-inelastic. These considerations suggest the hypothesis:

1. The Sylos Postulate will not apply as a description of reaction when an entrant combines large entry scale and larger relative parent company size.

Empirical observation suggests one qualification to this hypothesis. Muted reaction to larger entrants may not apply when incumbents draw a large percentage of their total sales from the entered market. In this case, incumbents have much more at stake—indeed, for the single product company, its very existence is at stake. An example[3] is the spaghetti sauce market, dominated by Ragu which draws almost all its total sales therefrom. When Heinz, Del Monte, and Campbell entered this market, Ragu reacted strongly with price cuts to, and frequently below, the competitive level. The "big three" withdrew. The qualification to hypothesis 1 is, therefore:

1a. The Sylos Postulate and Stiglerian Output Expansion will apply when an incumbent draws more than 50 percent of its total sales from the entered product-

---

3. Trade source of information.

> market, regardless of the entry scale and relative
> size of the entrant.

The influence of market characteristics other than concentration and number of sellers on postentry reaction by
incumbents has not been widely studied. A notable exception is the work of Marris (1968) who has studied the
influence of market growth. In chapter 2 above, it was
suggested that reaction might be less in a growth market
because the entrant does not have to displace incumbent
sales to achieve an adequate share. In effect, growth in an
oligopoly reduces strategic interdependence and moves
this structure closer to the perfect competition structure
insofar as rivals' conduct is concerned. Conversely, an entrant into a low-growth market must take sales from incumbents: as Marris (1968: 187) comments: "In static markets
the conflict situation is necessarily intense. . . . [An
entrant] may be compelled to fight a war in which one
or more producers is driven out to make room for him"
(p. 194).

Marris also (pp. 188–192) predicts that entrants into a
growth market will not experience competitive reaction
because incumbents know their "absolute sales are still
expanding," and they do not know how "their proportionate share is behaving." Eventually, however, incumbents
"realize their sales curve begins to look seriously un-
healthy" and then they react. War commences and Marris
assumes that the major weapon is price. War ends with
agreement on a "peace price"; that is, the price that "will
keep market shares constant." In summary, his argument
is that incumbents in a growth market faced with entry
will, first, delay reaction until their sales volume declines,
then fight back on price, and finally, stop fighting at a
"peace price."

Alemson (1969) takes exception to this view of reaction
in growth markets. First, he notes that a "wait and see"
approach by the incumbents is contradictory to Marris's
own theory that managers seek firm sales growth. If this
objective applies, Alemson argues, incumbents will surely
not lie low in the face of entry which could impair their

growth. This criticism is not entirely fair because Marris assumes that incumbents' sales volume continues to increase in a growth market, even after entry takes place; the decline that occurs is in their share. Second, he notes that the collecting of information is very sophisticated in the modern firm. Thus, it seems unlikely that incumbents would not know that their share has declined. This criticism is more to the point, not only because Alemson is right about the amount and type of information available to the modern firm but also because managers have been trained to think of their strategy in terms of its impact upon their market share. Although he does not say so, Alemson presumably expects reaction in growth markets to occur when incumbents' share declines. In effect, this view is also the view of Marris. This hypothesis seems entirely plausible, and Bevan's account (1974) of the UK potato crisp market provides one example where this did in fact occur.

The disagreements between these two researchers arise because each studies only part of the picture. If reaction in a growth market is dependent on incumbents' share loss, it then becomes necessary to study how share might be lost. One immediately obvious cause is the entry strategy chosen by the entrants. If an entrant offers a superior customer bargain, for example, the price cutter and higher quality combination discussed in chapter 9, then it would seem reasonable that incumbents will lose share, and eventually volume, if they do not match or better the entrant's offer. The likelihood of reaction in a growth market, therefore, would seem to be contingent upon share losses' occurring, which, in turn, is contingent upon the aggressiveness of the entrant's entry strategy.

This chain of reasoning does not necessarily mean that reaction will always occur in growth markets once share loss has been experienced. The first incumbent in the product-market started at 100 percent market share; few managers would expect this situation to continue and most would actually budget a declining share over time as the market matures. In the extreme case, the first incumbents may actually encourage entry as a means of defraying the costs of market development. RCA's licensing of other firms to make color television receivers is a ready example.

It remains an empirical matter to establish the level of incumbent share loss at which reaction occurs. Once it has occurred, Marris assumes reaction on price only and then a settlement for stable shares. Although the data in this study may not cover a sufficient time period to permit tests, it seems unlikely that rivals in growth markets will fight only on price or that they will settle for stable shares. While rivalry on price will obviously occur in growth markets (after any initial inelasticity has been exploited), it is necessary to recall that the rubric "growth markets" also usually means rapidly changing technology of production, product design, and means of distribution (discussed in chapter 2). Thus, rivalry in growth markets is likely to be multifaceted, on most or all elements of the marketing mix, as rivals respond to one another's attempts to find the most effective methods of operation. Furthermore, strategists in a growth market probably believe that the prize of market leader is still available to be won. This belief, together with market turmoil, seems likely to make even a price-share settlement through unconscious parallelism unlikely. It seems, therefore, that two conditions are necessary for the third stage of Marris's description of reaction in growth-markets—agreement on a "peace price"—to hold: first, a view among the relevant strategists that the market prize has been won; and second, market price elasticity has been exhausted. Although these two conditions are difficult to measure in practice, it is likely that they occur when the market growth rate has slowed. Thus, by this reasoning, Marris's third stage of reaction would occur only when the market condition to which he applies it no longer exists; that is, when the market has changed to a mature market.

Reaction in mature markets, if one accepts that equilibrium theorizing assumes a market condition similar to a mature market, is more extensively dealt with in the literature. As noted in chapter 8, most entrants in this sample entered growth markets, and this means that it will be almost impossible to test hypotheses about reaction in mature markets. It also means that, to the extent this sample is representative of all entry, most theorizing in the literature deals with a situation that occurs infrequently in practice.[4]

Marris separated reaction in a mature market from that in a growth market. Although his views are not entirely clear, he seems to suggest a "wait and see" pattern in mature markets similar to reaction in growth markets. But he also suggests that reaction in undifferentiated mature markets is likely to be immediate. He notes that entry into undifferentiated markets necessitates a high degree of imitation. However, the more the entrant imitates existing firms "the greater their incentive to fight him off" (p. 193). This view is contrary to Bain's (1956). He sees the lack of product differentiation barriers in an undifferentiated, mature oligopoly and concludes that entry costs are lower because the entrant does not have to overcome existing customer loyalties. To Bain, therefore, entry into an undifferentiated mature market is easy. This view overlooks the possibility expressed by Marris that imitation in a slow-growth market makes reaction necessary. Marris concludes that the entrants' costs would be higher because of the need to counter this reaction and these costs are "analogous to the marketing expenses in non-imitative diversification" (p. 193). Regardless, therefore, of whether a mature market is undifferentiated, this reasoning indicates that entry into a mature market seems more likely to provoke greater reaction than entry into a growth market. This reaction is likely to impair entrant performance, although by how much it is difficult to determine.

To summarize these arguments, it seems probable that reaction on the elements of the marketing mix to entry into growth markets will be less than in mature markets. However, output expansion by a majority of entrants seems likely, not necessarily as a response to entry but as a response to market growth. Incumbents' share may well decline in spite of this output expansion, possibly through

---

4. It is possible that entry into mature markets might be more prevalent in a sample of acquisitions (although such a sample may not meet the definition of entry presented here in chapter 1).

ignorance but also through a realization that share above some levels is not usually maintained, or through a desire to lower market development costs. Share declines can be tested, but the different explanations for declines of course cannot be tested.

It has also been suggested that magnitude of reaction may be linked to incumbents' share losses. It is not clear, however, at what level of share loss reaction will occur. This point suggests the existence of some threshhold level at which incumbents become alarmed and react. Thereafter, it seems likely that the magnitude of reaction increases directly with the magnitude of share loss. Eventually, reaction magnitude will decline as incumbents conclude that their share loss is so large to be irrecoverable.

At least one cause of incumbents' share loss is likely to be the entrant's strategy. The better the customer bargain offered, the more likely it is that incumbents will lose share unless they react. Marris's argument about reaction on price only was not accepted, and it is expected that incumbents can react on price, capacity, product, marketing expenditures, and distribution.

The following hypotheses seem amenable to test with this study's data:

2. Entrants into growth markets will report a lower index of reaction than entrants into mature markets.
3. Most incumbents in growth markets continue to increase output after entry but show share losses in the first two years of entry.
4. Reaction will be higher as incumbents' share loss between pre- and postentry periods is larger.
5. Incumbents' share loss rises as entrant's strategy becomes aggressive: inversely with relative price, and positively with relative quality, length of line, and breadth of segment.

THE DATA

Table 56 shows the number of entrants that believed reaction occurred as a direct result of their entry during

TABLE 56. RESPONDENTS' JUDGMENTS ABOUT COMPETITIVE
REACTION AS A DIRECT RESULT OF THEIR ENTRY

	Entrants	
	Number	Percent
No reaction on any element of marketing mix	17	46
Reaction on at least one element of marketing mix	20	54
	37	100

Breakdown of Reaction by Elements of Marketing Mix		
Price		
Decrease greater than 25%	2	5
Decrease 6–15%	1	5
Decrease 1–5%	5	14
No reaction	28	76
Price increase	1	3
	37	100
Product		
Changes to match entrant's product	9	24
No changes	27	73
Changes that helped entrant's relative advantage	1	3
	37	100
Marketing Expenditures		
Increases beyond entrant's expenditures	6	16
Increases to match entrant's expenditures	6	16
No change in incumbent's expenditures	25	68
Decrease in incumbent's expenditures	0	0
	37	100
Capacity Changes		
Incumbents increased capacity greater than 30%	1	3
Incumbents increased capacity 11–20%	2	5
Incumbents increased capacity 1–10%	7	19
No capacity increases	25	68
Incumbents reduced capacity	2	5
	37	100
Distribution Changes		
Matched entrants distribution method	4	11
No change in distribution method	33	89
	37	100
Parent Company Rivalry	No	Yes
Parent companies of incumbents launch start-up businesses against other components of your company?	37	0

the first two years. Of the thirty-seven entrants with complete data on the reaction questions seventeen, or 45 percent, reported no reaction at all, and twenty reported reaction on at least one item of the marketing mix. The table also shows reaction by individual elements of the marketing mix. No reaction is the most common response by an overwhelming margin: 73 percent reported no reaction on price, 73 percent on product changes, 68 percent on marketing expenditures, 68 percent on capacity additions, and 89 percent on distribution changes.

Respondents also judged that their parent companies experienced no invasion in their other markets from the parent companies of incumbents, in the first two years of entry. It is possible that the period of two years is insufficient to analyze, organize and implement a counterinvasion entry. If true, the finding in this study of no counterinvasion should be interpreted as indicating that counterinvasion is unlikely to occur within the first two years rather than that it will not occur.[5]

The mean index of reaction percentage reported by entrant business managers was 6 percent and the median level of reaction was 2 percent (see table 57). About three-quarters of the sample, 76 percent, recorded an index of reaction of 10 percent or less.

Incumbents' policy on output was traced by relating competitors' market shares, as judged by entrant business managers, to the size of the total market, in the year prior to entry and in the first two years of entry. Table 58 shows that a majority of incumbents, twenty out of thirty-three with complete annual share data, or 61 percent, increased their annual output in the first two years of entry over their annual output in the year prior to entry.

However, in spite of volume increases for the majority of the sample, the top three competitors in a majority of entered product-markets lost market share (see table 59). Of thirty-three entered product-markets, the top three

---

5. Knickerbocker (1973) used periods of three, five, and seven years and varied the period according to country. Longer periods seem likely to increase the number of occurrences of counterinvasion but make analysis of the causes of such counterinvasion more difficult, particularly with a small sample. In contrast, Knickerbocker's sample was 187.

TABLE 57. DISTRIBUTION OF
SAMPLE ON THE INDEX OF
REACTION

	Entrants	
	Number	*Percent*
0%	17	46
1–5%	6	16
6–10%	5	14
11–15%	2	5
16–20%	5	14
21%	2	5
	37	100

Mean 6%; (Standard deviation
8%); Median 2%

competitors in twenty-two of these, or 67 percent, lost more than 1 percent in share. The bulk of this loss occurred in the first year of entry. The bar chart in figure 7 shows that the top three combined share in the year before entry averaged 67 percent but dropped to 56 percent in the first year of entry, and then stayed around 52 percent thereafter.

These share losses were not proportionately spread over the top three competitors. Indeed, it seems as if the largest competitor prior to entry suffered severe share losses and the second and third largest competitors, based on preentry sales, sometimes increased their share (see figure 8).

HYPOTHESIS TESTING

The data in table 58 showing that incumbents in two markets maintained volume means that hypotheses 1 and

TABLE 58. COMPARISON OF PRE- AND POSTENTRY
OUTPUT OF TOP THREE COMPETITORS

Top Three Competitors	*Number of Entered Markets*
Increased output	20
Decreased output	11
Showed no change	2
	33

TABLE 59. BREAKDOWN OF TOP THREE COMPETITORS' SHARE CHANGES BETWEEN FIRST TWO YEARS OF ENTRY AND YEAR PRIOR TO ENTRY

Top Three Competitors	Number of Entered Markets
Lost more than ten points per share	11
Lost up to ten points per share	11
No change in share/increased share	11
	33

1a involving the Sylos Postulate cannot be tested. More generally, it seems that the Sylos Postulate describes the rare case of competitive reaction, according to this sample of entrants and incumbents.

It is interesting to trace through the different price-output reactions by incumbents, both for its own value and as a basis for future theorizing. Of the twenty-eight entrants who reported that incumbents did not react on price, nine estimated that the incumbents decreased output and nineteen estimated that incumbents increased output. An attempt was made to see if decreases in incumbents' output were associated with lower entry scales, following Wenders's theorizing above that small-scale entrants would be accepted. In the nine cases of reduced output, four entrants had an entry production scale below the median entry scale of 22 percent and five exceeded this amount.

FIGURE 7. AVERAGE SHARE OF TOP THREE COMPETITORS PRIOR TO ENTRY AND IN FIRST FOUR YEARS OF ENTRY

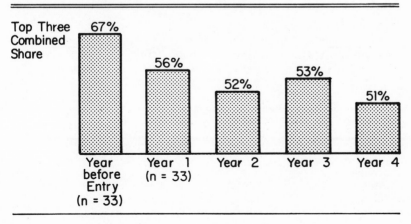

FIGURE 8. AVERAGE SHARE OF LARGEST COMPETITOR IN THE YEAR
PRIOR TO ENTRY AND IN THE FIRST FOUR YEARS OF ENTRY

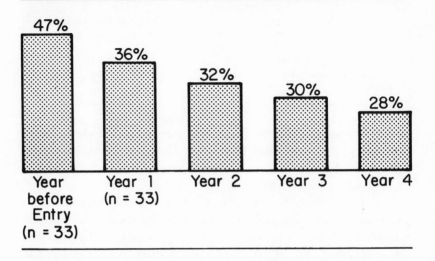

Market growth, or the lack thereof, seems a much more likely explanation of the decreases in output. Table 60 shows that the growth rate in markets where incumbents decreased output was significantly lower than that in markets where incumbents increased output. These data suggest that incumbents in lower growth markets are likely to reduce output and allow the entrant to take up the output forsaken and any extra output from market growth rather than maintain output and experience a price decrease. When demand is inelastic with respect to price, as it is likely to be in low-growth markets, this reaction is not irrational.

TABLE 60. MARKET GROWTH AND OUTPUT CHANGES AMONG
INCUMBENTS SHOWING NO REACTION ON PRICE

	No Reaction on Price ($n = 28$)		
Five-Year Served Market Growth Rate	*Incumbents Decreased Output (Percent) ($n = 9$)*	*Incumbents Increased Output (Percent) ($n = 19$)*	*Probability*
Mean	8	43	0.02
Median	4	17	

Of the eight entrants who judged that incumbents dropped their prices as a result of entry, three estimated that the incumbents decreased output and five estimated that they increased output. One point that does emerge from these data and the literature review for hypothesis 1 is that Stigler's idea of output expansion is much closer to the behavior reported by this sample. Again, however, in most cases, expansion of output did not result in lower prices, as predicted by Stigler, because significant market growth occurred.

Hypotheses 2–5 can be tested on these data. Table 61 shows that hypothesis 2—a lower index of reaction in growth markets—is not supported by the data. Reaction is significantly lower in the mature stage at 1 percent than in growth, 6 percent, and introductory stages, 10 percent. Reaction is also significantly lower in markets growing at less than 10 percent annually compared with those growing faster than 10 percent.

At this stage, hypothesis 4 should be recalled—higher reaction as share loss increases. Table 62 shows that incumbents in markets judged to be in the introductory stage lost more share in the first two years of entry than incumbents in markets judged to be mature. For example, comparing incumbents pre- and postentry means that those in

TABLE 61. INDEX OF REACTION BY STAGE OF PRODUCT LIFE
CYCLE AND GROWTH RATE

Percentage Index of Reaction	Stage of Product Life Cycle			
	Introductory (n = 10)	Growth (n = 21)	Mature (n = 6)	Probability
Mean	10	6	1	Introductory vs. Growth = 0.15 Introductory vs. Mature = 0.01 Mature vs. Growth = 0.01
Median	8	1	0	

	Five-Year Served Market Growth Rate		
	10% or More (n = 28)	Less than 10% (n = 9)	Probability
Mean	8	2	0.01
Median	3	0	

TABLE 62. INCUMBENTS' PRE- AND POSTENTRY SHARE BY STAGE OF PRODUCT LIFE CYCLE AND GROWTH RATE

Percentage Incumbents' Share	Stage of Product Life Cycle					
	Mean			Median		
	Introductory (n = 9)	Growth (n = 21)	Mature (n = 5)	Introductory (n = 9)	Growth (n = 21)	Mature (n = 5)
Preentry	59	69	66	65	68	63
Postentry	43	61	61	45	62	55
Share loss	16	8	5	20	6	8

Five-Year Served Market Growth Rate

	Mean		Median	
	More Than 10%	Less Than 10%	More Than 10%	Less Than 10%
Preentry	68	60	65	63
Postentry	57	55	54	63
Share loss	11	5	11	0

introductory markets lost 16 share points, whereas those in mature markets lost 5 share points. The medians show a similar pattern.

Hypothesis 4 is tested directly in table 63. Incumbents who lost more than 10 points of share recorded a significantly higher index of reaction than those who either gained share or showed no change in share. However, there is an insignificant difference among the three groups of share change. This fact makes the evidence weaker. The medians exhibit the threshhold behavior reported earlier: a median of no reaction up to 10 points loss in share, thereafter a median reaction of 7 percent. The data suggest that hypothesis 4 should not be rejected but more evidence is needed for a stronger conclusion.

Data in tables 64 and 65 suggest that hypothesis 3—most incumbents in growth markets increase output but lose share—should not be rejected. Table 64 shows the output and share changes for incumbents divided into two groups: those in markets with an average annual growth rate greater than 10 percent per year and those in markets growing at 10 percent or less. Twenty-eight entered markets had average annual growth greater than 10 percent and, in twenty-two of these, incumbents increased output in the first two years of entry compared with their preentry output, and six decreased output. It seems that incumbents in most of these twenty-eight markets did not increase output enough because they lost share in twenty (or 79 percent) of the markets; only four gained share, and four showed no share change.

Data in table 65 test hypothesis 3 directly by breaking

TABLE 63. INDEX OF REACTION BY INCUMBENTS' SHARE CHANGE BETWEEN PRE- AND POSTENTRY YEARS

Percentage Index of Reaction	Incumbents' Gained Share/ No Share Change (n = 12)	Incumbents' Lost up to Ten Points (n = 12)	Incumbents' Lost More Than Ten Points (n = 11)	Probability
Mean	4	6	8	Column 1 vs. column 3 = 0.10
Median	0	0	7	

TABLE 64. TOP THREE COMPETITORS' OUTPUT AND SHARE
CHANGE BETWEEN PREENTRY YEAR AND FIRST TWO
POSTENTRY YEARS BY SERVED MARKET GROWTH RATE

	Five-Year[a] Served Market Average Growth Rate		
Output Changes	More Than 10% (n = 28)	10% or Less (n = 9)	Total
Increased output	22	3	25
Decreased output	6	6	12
	28	9	37

Chi squared value (Yates correction) significant at 0.03

Share Changes			
Lost share	20	4	24
Gained (4)/ no change (4)	8	4	12
	28	8[b]	36

[a] Average three years prior to entry and first two years of entry.
[b] One missing value on share data.

down the twenty-five markets in which incumbents increased output into two rates of market growth and two types of share change. Incumbents in fourteen markets growing at more than 10 percent annually lost share, in contrast to eight in which their share increased or did not change. In contrast, no incumbents in markets growing at 10 percent or less lost share. The chi-squared value reaches a 0.07 level of significance, which suggests, al-

TABLE 65. BREAKDOWN OF MARKETS IN WHICH INCUMBENTS
INCREASED OUTPUT BY AVERAGE GROWTH RATE AND
INCUMBENTS' SHARE CHANGE

Incumbents that Increased Output (n = 25)	Five-Year Market Average Growth Rate		
	More Than 10% (n = 22)	10% or Less (n = 3)	Total
Lost share	14	0	14
Gained (4)/no change (4)	8	3	11
	22	3	25

Chi squared value (Yates correction) significant at 0.07

though not as strongly as one would hope, that the hypothesis should not be rejected out of hand.

Hypothesis 5—that incumbents' share loss is greater as entrant's price is lower, quality is higher, and length of time is broader—does not seem to be rejected by the data. Table 66 shows three groups of incumbents' share change and the entry strategy they faced. Incumbents who gained share or showed no change faced entrants with a product quality rating of 22 percent, whereas those who lost more than 10 points faced entrants with 58 percent. Similarly, the larger the production entry scale of the entrant, the greater incumbents' share loss.

The table also shows that incumbents who lost more than 10 points in share were more likely to face entrants with a strategy of offering a broader line and serving more customers. For example, of the eleven incumbents who did not lose share, only one faced an entrant with a broader line and none faced an entrant who served a larger seg-

TABLE 66. ENTRANTS' STRATEGY AND INCUMBENTS' SHARE
CHANGE

	Incumbents' (Top Three) Share Change in First Two Years Compared with Preentry Share		
Entrants	*Incumbents Gained or No Share Change (n = 11)*	*Incumbents Lost Up to Ten Points (n = 11)*	*Incumbents Lost More Than Ten Points (n = 11)*
Relative quality	23%	30%	58%
Capacity as percentage of market	8%	51%	70%
Length of line Number of entrants broader line	1	1	5
Number of entrants narrower line[a]	7	8	5
Size of segment Number of entrants larger segment	0	3	5
Number of entrants smaller segment[a]	0	1	0
Relative price	1.47	1.32	1.15

[a] Number of entrants similar to competition not shown.

ment. In contrast, of the eleven incumbents who lost more than 10 share points, five faced entrants with a broader line and five faced entrants who served a larger segment.

Incumbents who did not lose share faced entrants whose average relative price was 1.47, but those who lost more than 10 share points faced an average relative price of 1.15.

Finally, table 67 suggests that reaction occurred when the entrant's strategy offered higher quality and was more ambitious. For example, the average relative product quality offered by entrants who reported no reaction from incumbents was 21 percent, whereas for those who reported some reaction, it was 55 percent. Similarly, entrants who reported some reaction entered with a larger production scale and were more likely to offer a broader line and serve a larger segment.

The primary generalization emerging from this presentation of data and testing of hypotheses is that the level of reaction is more likely to be determined by incumbents' magnitude of share loss than by whether the entered market is in a growth or mature stage. In turn, share loss is partially influenced by the quality to the customer of the entrant's strategy. Incumbents' share loss is greatest when

TABLE 67. ENTRANTS' STRATEGY AND THE INDEX OF REACTION

Entrants	No Reaction (Index = 0) (n = 16)	Some Reaction (Index = 1-27%) (n = 20)
Relative quality	21%	55%
Capacity as percentage of market	23%	49%
Length of line		
Number of entrants broader line	1	6
Number of entrants narrower line	11	12
Size of segment		
Number of entrants larger segment	1	6
Number of entrants smaller segment	12	11
Relative price	1.30	1.30

[a] Number of entrants similar to competition not shown.

TABLE 68. PERFORMANCE MEASURES BY THE INDEX OF REACTION, FIRST TWO YEARS

Percentage Performance Measures		No Reaction (Index = 0) (n = 16)	Some Reaction (Index = 1–27%) (n = 20)	Probability (< 0.2)
Cash flow/investment ($R^2 = 0.07$)	Mean	−79	−106	0.05
	Median	−68	−80	
Return on investment ($R^2 = 0.05$)	Mean	−39	−77	0.10
	Median	−40	−32	
Return on sales ($R^2 = 0.02$)	Mean	−61	−96	0.18
	Median	−37	−73	
Relative price/cost ($R^2 = 0.03$)	Mean	0.88	0.96	0.16
	Median	0.98	1.00	
Relative share ($R^2 = 0.08$)	Mean	25	59	0.05
	Median	10	23	

the entrant offers a higher quality, a lower price, a broader line, and serves a larger segment. Although incumbents increased output, most did not do so in sufficient magnitude to prevent significant share losses. It cannot be determined from these data whether the failure to hold share was a conscious decision by the incumbents or was caused solely by the quality of the entrant's strategy.

PERFORMANCE AND REACTION

In chapter 2, it was considered that the level of reaction would be an important influence on entrant business performance. Financial and market performance data presented by the index of reaction (table 68) suggest that entrants who reported no reaction as a result of their entry did somewhat better on financial performance than those who experienced reaction. For example, entrants who experienced no reaction recorded a cash flow/investment ratio of −79 percent, compared with −106 percent for those against incumbents who did react; similar differences exist for the ROI measure and return on sales, although the significance probability on the latter at 0.18 is high.

The reverse picture is presented on market performance. Entrants who experienced reaction held a relative market share of 59 percent, significantly higher than the 25 percent held by entrants who experienced no reaction. It is important to emphasize, however, that the R^2 on all measures are among the lowest yet seen. This result seems to be in accord with the data showing a low absolute level of reaction but contrary to the theoretical expectations laid out in chapters 1 and 2. This fact, plus low differences among the means and medians, suggests that entrants' problems, as seen in chapters 4 and 5, cannot be attributed to the intensity of reaction from incumbents.

11. Summary of Findings and Implications

IT IS AN UNDERSTATEMENT to say that this study demonstrates that entry into product-markets where a firm has not previously competed is difficult. Negative financial performance as large as seen in the study sample, and for as long as eight years according to the PIMS sample, cannot be among the more attractive investment opportunities facing established firms. And, it should be recalled from chapter 3, the entrants in both samples are survivors. This factor means, presumably, that the performance of a sample of *all* entrant businesses launched would be even worse. Furthermore, these entrant businesses were started by highly diversified and large (*Fortune* top 200) companies. It seems reasonable to assume that these firms employ managers who are among the more experienced at dealing with diverse product-markets. To the extent that this assumption is true, these results further underline the difficulty of entry.

An alternative explanation may be that experience in diversity does not transfer to new diversifications, even within the same corporation or the same division. Is each entrant business launched by an established firm a new experience, at least for the managers in charge of implementing the entry? It will be recalled from chapter 1 that this possibility has generally not been assumed in the literature. Indeed, the relatedness concept in the analytical framework explicitly assumed some degree of experience transfer (and the findings in chapter 7 on that concept indicated that this hypothesis was not unlikely). At the same time, of course, the analytical framework did suggest that relatedness by itself was not enough—the market entered, the entry strategy chosen, and the reaction experienced play a role, too. The findings in the chapters on these other concepts indicate that this view is also not unreasonable.

What, then, as a summary statement, can be said about the magnitude and duration of the financial losses and the unimpressive median share recorded by this sample of entrants? In large part, I judge that their poor performance was self-inflicted. In effect, these entrants obtained the market share they deserved, and this in turn contributed to their poor financial performance. To recall chapter 9, the predominant entry strategy of the entrants studied consisted of relatively shorter product lines, narrower served market segments, lower marketing expenditures, higher prices, and better quality than incumbents. In other words, most of these entrants did not have a strategy with as broad a served market appeal as their competitors; naturally enough, they achieved a lower relative share than these rivals. And then, as they tried to build share through their first four years, their financial performance suffered from the extra costs; apart from which, it will be recalled from chapter 5, the amount of absolute share increase was small. The reason for this result seems to be that many entrants were in markets with quite extraordinary growth rates. Thus, in spite of impressive growth in their own sales revenues, continued total market growth prevented any significant share improvement.

I also believe that these results, apart from being self-inflicted, were consciously planned—at least in terms of market share. Most entrants claimed that they targeted a low initial share of market. Table 69 shows that nineteen entrants, or 51 percent of the sample that provided share objectives data, had a market share objective in the first two years below 10 percent.

In the light of these low share objectives, the predominant choice of strategy seems to have been appropriate. A good match between share objectives and entry strategy, however, was not sufficient, in itself, to prevent financial

TABLE 69. MARKET SHARE OBJECTIVES AND SHARE
ACHIEVED, FIRST TWO YEARS

Share Range Objective	Number of Entrants	Actual Share	
		Achieved Objective	Missed Objective
Up to 5%	16	4	12
6–10%	3	2	1
11–15%	7	2	5
16–20%	5	4	1
20%+	6	3	3
	37	15	22

losses. In addition, most entrants, twenty-two or 59 percent
of the sample, did not achieve their share objectives (see
table 69). It appears, therefore, that low initial share was
a conscious decision. Surely, the negative financial results
were not conscious but, the moment managers decided to
seek a toe-hold in their served market, they had, in effect,
preordained them.

Turning from the facts of entry to explaining the observed performance, we can say that the variables in the
analytical framework presented in chapter 1 and expanded
in chapter 2 provide considerable insight. Unfortunately,
the small sample size, the wide dispersion of several distributions, and the skewness of other distributions make
rigorous explanation and estimation of relationships impossible. What began as a large data base, model-building
project with the objective of developing "laws of entry"
ended up as a small sample, part numerate–part case project with the more limited goal of developing insights useful to executives.

The most disappointing feature of the explanatory chapters was the need to analyze the impact of each variable
individually. Obviously, explaining business performance
is a multivariate problem, but I have not been able to
formally do that. On the other hand, I believe I can do it
on an informal basis. One advantage of a small sample size
is that the researcher can examine individual observations.
I have done this extensively; further, I have talked with
the managers of many of the entrant businesses in this

sample. Given the importance of a multivariate analysis and my knowledge of the sample, it seems appropriate to link the variables together on a judgmental basis. We turn to this analysis now. Our starting point is the data in table 70 which shows the number of entrants or median percentages of selected variables organized by type of relatedness.

Forward integration and technology entrants had many characteristics in common. They were both more likely to have entered markets in an earlier stage of development than marketing entrants, and both were in more rapid growth markets than marketing entrants. Both claimed incremental innovations, whereas most marketing entrants offered an imitation. Both had high R&D/sales ratios. In short, both were early entrants into a product-market and were, therefore, involved in a market development task. Thereafter, the similarities end. Forward integration entrants offered the lowest quality, had the highest marketing/sales ratio, obtained the most inferior relative price-cost bargain, experienced the greatest amount of competitive reaction, and had the lowest capacity utilization.

As was seen in chapter 7, forward integration entrants performed poorly, assuming that the parent company was not taking a profit elsewhere in the line. The characteristics above suggest some of their problems. At the same time, the fact that forward integration entrants offered incremental innovations and suffered the most negative performance throughout the first four years explains some of the apparently inferior performance of the incremental innovators versus similar offering entrants (chapter 9). The former group, it transpires, contained at least two types of entrants: those who were improving their performance—technology entrants—and those—the forward integration entrants—who were not improving their performance.

The different performance exhibited by forward integration and technology entrants is curious and, potentially, an important finding. After all, it seems that they were trying an essentially similar mode of entry (that is, based on an incremental innovation) and yet one showed progress while the other did not. There is at least one known dif-

TABLE 70. TYPE OF RELATEDNESS BY OTHER SELECTED VARIABLES IN THE ANALYTICAL FRAMEWORK, FIRST TWO YEARS

Number of Entrants in Each Category

Type of Relatedness	Product Life Cycle			Degree of Innovation		Length of Line			Number of Customers		
	Introductory	Growth	Mature	Increased Innovation	Similar Offer	L	S	B[a]	L	S	M[b]
Forward integration (n = 7)	3	4	0	5	2	4	0	3	6	1	0
Technology (n = 10)	4	4	2	10	0	8	1	1	7	1	2
Marketing (n = 12)	0	10	2	4	8	6	3	3	7	3	2

Median Percentage of Each Type of Relatedness

	Five-Year Growth Rate	Product Entry Scale	Relative Quality	Relative Price Cost	Relative Price	Relative Cost	Capital Utilization	Reaction
Forward integration (n = 7)	35	13	33	0.88	1.05	1.04	27	10
Technology (n = 10)	38	21	70	0.97	1.03	1.20	47	6
Marketing (n = 12)	25	9	50	1.00	1.05	1.08	64	0

[a] L = Less broad; S = Similar breadth; B = Broader.
[b] L = Less; S = About the same; M = More.

ference between the two. Forward integration entrants, by definition, did not benefit from parent company technical knowledge. They also reported the lowest familiarity with the R&D and manufacturing skills in the entered market. It does not seem unreasonable to conjecture that lack of in-house technical knowledge, together with the new marketing conditions faced in the forward market, created a severe handicap.

The basis of the forward integration type of relatedness is a high proportion of inputs purchased within the parent company. Thus, these entrants combined lack of technical and marketing knowledge with high knowledge of parent company inputs. This combination of factors, together with their apparent inferior performance, suggests that knowledge of a component or a material is a poor basis on which to plan an entry if technical backing on what to do with that input in the entered market and marketing knowledge on how to design, price, service, and sell products in that entered market are lacking.

Another difference between the two types is that forward integration entrants are much more likely to be competing with former customers than technology entrants. This factor may partially explain why forward integration entrants experienced the highest index of reaction.

These findings about forward integration entrants have important implications for the corporate strategy decision to integrate toward the customer. This strategy is one of the major options available to established firms, particularly those in the petrochemicals, steel, metals, rubber, and paper industries. For example, a recent *Fortune* article (1976) included the observation: "Ask the head of any major chemical company where his profit future lies and he will unhesitatingly respond: as close to the consumer as I can get" (p. 98). In the same article, Mr. Z. D. Bonner, president of Gulf Oil Chemicals, was quoted as saying: "Obviously, the further you can go toward the customer, the better it is. We had a very bad experience in plastic bags. Next time we will be more careful in choosing a product and a market" (p. 156). Enough of these "bad experiences" within an established firm can of course be sufficient to depress the performance of the entire firm.

Indeed, Rumelt (1974) found that established firms with the dominant vertical corporate strategy, in contrast to those with diversification corporate strategies, achieved the lowest levels of financial performance (chaps. 3, 4). The dominant vertical corporate strategy is the strategy that would produce the highest relative frequency of vertical integration entrants.

Technology entrants offered the highest level of quality of any of the three types, but they also suffered the greatest relative cost disadvantage and obtained the lowest premium over incumbents on their relative prices (1.03, compared with 1.05 for forward integration and marketing entrants). They showed a stronger tendency than the other two entrants to offer a narrower product line. On their operating and capital ratios, it will be recalled that they had the highest R&D/sales revenues and investment/sales revenues ratios of all three types of relatedness. Technology entrants had the highest median entry production scale, which may partially explain their high investment/sales revenues ratio. In view of having the highest production scale, at 21 percent, their median capacity utilization at 47 percent was quite impressive. Presumably, this combination of features helps to explain their superior relative share performance.

These considerations suggest that there need be much less concern about the techology related type of entrant. They were involved in an incrementally innovative mode of entry, bearing part of the costs of market development, and yet showed superior share performance and an improving financial performance. I conjecture that part of their severe cost disadvantage came from offering such a high level of relative product quality. For example, of the seven technology entrants at a direct cost disadvantage, five offered a relative product well above (to be more precise, about 50–70 points higher) the PIMS established business quality level of 24 percent. Furthermore, these entrants did not obtain significantly higher relative prices for their higher relative quality. It seems reasonable to conclude tentatively, therefore, that technology entrants misjudged either the premium that customers would pay for higher quality or the quality level that customers desired. If the first misjudgment applies, then they could have charged higher prices. If the second applies, then they could have lowered quality. Either way some improvement in financial performance could have been achieved and, depending on individual demand sensitivities to price or quality, possibly at no cost to share performance.

The marketing entrants in this sample entered somewhat later in the product life cycle than forward integration or technology entrants: ten in the growth stage, two in the mature stage, and none in the introductory stage. The median growth rate of the market that they entered, at 25 percent, was also some 10 to 13 points lower than for the other two types. Most also offered an imitative product. Later and imitative entry amounts to a market penetration task, as opposed to the early and incrementally innovative entry of forward integration and technology entrants, which was termed a primarily market development task. The timing and mode of entry presumably meant that marketing entrants found that production technology, product design, and market acceptance were more developed. These benefits should have lowered their operating and capital ratios, from lower absolute expenses on manufacturing or from higher absolute sales revenues or from a combination of both. Indeed, this result is exactly what was noted in chapter 7.

Marketing entrants' median product quality, at 50 percent, was clearly superior to incumbents' and was midway between that offered by forward integration and technology entrants. Their relative price-cost bargain was exactly at parity with incumbents' (1.00), which was the best performance by any of the three types of entrants. This achievement appears to have risen from charging slightly higher prices (median 1.05) and a relative cost disadvantage that was not too severe (median 1.08).

It is interesting to note that marketing entrants experienced the lowest median index of reaction. One interpretation of this result is that imitative entry into a still rapidly growing market is the least likely to generate incumbent reaction. The entrant has not set new standards to which incumbents might think reaction is necessary to maintain their ability to compete. And, in markets growing at 25 percent per year, incumbents seem less likely to perceive the entrant as a threat to their output levels. In contrast, forward integration and technology entrants did set new standards, because they offered incremental innovations, and some reaction might be considered appropriate in order to maintain competitiveness.

An alternative, or additional, explanation for low reaction might be that marketing entrants entered with the lowest median production scale of the three types (9 percent). Thus, incumbents may have calculated that the potential share gain by these entrants was not significant. The data in table 70 also suggest, however, that a higher percentage of marketing entrants offered similar or longer relative product lines and had a relatively greater number of customers. Entry marketing scale, therefore, was somewhat greater for marketing entrants than for forward integration and technology entrants. Nevertheless, from incumbents' point of view, the maximum threat to their output level lies in the entrant's production scale, and this was generally not significant.

The general impression from this combination of marketing relatedness with the other concepts in the analytical framework is that they had their entry much more under control. They did not exhibit extreme values, either on their operating or capital ratios or on their strategy. For example, they did not offer vastly superior product quality, as did technology entrants; not one of them had a very severe cost disadvantage; and none recorded R&D/sales revenue or marketing/sales revenue ratios above 60 percent.

I would suggest three reasons for the greater control and better performance shown by marketing entrants. The first two are their later entry and imitative entry already mentioned. Marris (1964) termed this type of entry "bandwaggoning" and predicted that, in a growth market, it could be very successful. The evidence from this sample appears to support this view. The third reason is their greater knowledge of customers. By definition, marketing entrants were able to draw on existing customers of the parent company to a much greater extent than the other two types of entrant.

The various concepts have now been related as far as I think it is justifiable to take these data and sample size. An interesting omission is the market structure variable: no discernible relationship between this variable and type of relatedness appeared. It will be recalled, however, that entrants into loose oligopolies recorded better performance than entrants into tight or moderate oligopolies. This variable, therefore, appears to have some independent influence on performance: that is, its influence may not be contingent on the levels of other variables.

IMPLICATIONS FOR MANAGEMENT

The major normative suggestion emerging from this study, in my opinion, is that entry on a large scale is necessary for eventual success in rapid growth markets. Entry scale here refers to both production and marketing scale. One reason for this suggestion is that an annual market growth of 50 percent—about the average reported for markets entered in this sample—means that an entrant's maximum *potential* share, based on production capacity, is halved each year. That is, an entrant with a capacity equivalent to a 25 percent market share at the beginning of the year in a market growing at 50 percent per year, has a capacity equivalent to a 17 percent share at the end of the year. Of course, incremental increases in scale during the early years of entry are possible, but, judging by this sample, these were not frequent occurrences. The average performance of this sample in the first two years of entry probably explains why: it cannot be an easy management decision to double capacity when viewing an ROI in the first two years of entry of −78 percent, even if the market is growing at 50 percent per year.

This problem raises a second normative suggestion. Managers should evaluate entrant businesses more on the basis of relative share achieved. In the short run, achieving a strong share position usually damages financial performance. In an effort to improve financial performance, management may reduce discretionary expenditures such as marketing and R&D or limit further investment. These decisions could result in the entrant's remaining at a low market share and, therefore, cause the continuance of the adverse financial performance.

A related suggestion is to use capitalized ROI for internal analysis of entrant businesses. Reliance on conventional measures of financial performance can seriously bias the evaluation of a new business, particularly if new businesses have to compete with established businesses for resources. Given that the initial heavy R&D and marketing expenses are meant to build a position for the future, capitalization brings the financial statements of a new business closer to those of established businesses.

Focusing on relative share and capitalized ROI would produce a better ordering of priorities and aid long-run decision making. The short-run goal for entrant businesses should be to obtain a strong relative share position—about 25 percent or more (ratio of entrant to top three competitors)—within the first four years. If the entrant is close to a positive capitalized ROI in the first four years as well as achieving 25 percent relative share, performance could be considered satisfactory.

It is recognized that the suggestion to enter on a more ambitious scale might appear foolhardy in view of the financial results reported in chapter 4. Such a suggestion would seem to promise only worse results, not better. This outcome may well be true—in the short run. In the long run, however, financial results should improve more quickly. Indeed, it is possible that the eight-year period taken to reach positive net income, on average, would be reduced significantly if a higher relative share position were achieved in the early years. Larger financial losses in the first two years in order to obtain higher relative share is likely to be a better long-run bargain than smaller losses and lower relative share.

Nevertheless, many managers, on reading chapter 4, will wonder whether entry should be considered at all. Certainly, it does not seem good personal strategy to seek the job of starting up a new business for the parent company.

Given short job durations, most managers would have been transferred, or dismissed, before their entrant business had approached positive net income. Senior level managers also have reason for concern. Just how many entrants can they afford and how patient can they be? Their answers to these questions are partially influenced by interest rates and the capital market. Rising interest rates, which appear in the denominator of discounting techniques, lower the estimated present value of an investment and, in turn, enhance the likelihood that managers will not go ahead with a new entrant or persevere with an existing entrant business. The capital market, in an era of quarterly earnings forecasts and frequent corporate scrutiny by financial analysts, appears to be emphasizing short-run financial performance. And yet, this emphasis is the prescription for unsatisfactory entrant business performance in the long run. The results reported here, therefore, appear to contain the potential to alter unfavorably the corporate environment in which new entry proposals are evaluated. There is a danger that managers' enthusiasm for entry activity will be seriously curtailed. While recognizing the basis of such a reaction, I would argue in favor of an alternative response.

A compromise response to these negative results, and to the normative implication to enter on a larger scale, is to start fewer entrant businesses but fund each on a more adequate basis. The increased level of resources might, as hypothesized above, be sufficient to produce positive net profits before year eight. Furthermore, if it is assumed that entry success is not a random process, there must be insights by which the seriously negative financial performance seen in chapter 4 can be improved. This research is a first step in identifying those insights and to them the chapter now turns.

The implications emerging from application of the analytical framework are several. Executives planning forward integration entrants should not assume that parent company strength in a material or a component is a sufficient basis for successful entry. Technical and marketing knowledge relevant to the entered market are very important.

Managers with this knowledge should be hired before the entrant business is launched. For example, in the case of Gulf and plastic bags cited earlier, it is unlikely that the petrochemicals executives were familiar with mass-merchandising retailers, pull promotion strategies, and information sources such as A. C. Nielsen and SAMI (without which few consumer marketing executives would attempt an entry). It is probable that this knowledge could have made a difference to Gulf's forward integration entry into plastic bags.

The data in chapter 8 suggested that managers could improve their initial results by entering markets in their growth stage (at which marketing entrants were particularly adept). It also appeared that the loose oligopoly market structure and a growth rate between 6 percent and 20 percent were associated with superior performance. These findings are useful guidelines that managers could include in their diversification/entry criteria.

In choosing an entry strategy, the first point that managers should address is their posture. Entry scale is one element of posture and the apparent need for larger entry scale has already been discussed. On two other elements of posture—relative innovation and forward integration—the data appear to suggest that imitation and relative forward integration greater than competitors'[1] lead to earlier superior performance. However, in the case of relative innovation, the median financial performance of incremental innovators was not substantially lower than the imitators and their relative share was higher. By no means, therefore, would it be appropriate to argue for imitative entry. Rather, the choice would appear to depend on the parent company's skills and the timing of entry. One speculation is that those established firms with a distinctive competence in technology are best suited to an incrementally innovative and early entry. Another speculation is that established firms with a marketing competence are

---

1. The term *forward integration* is used in two ways. First, there is a forward integration type of relatedness between the entrant business and its parent company. Second, there is the degree of forward integration of an entrant business relative to incumbents already operating in the entered product-market.

best suited to an imitative and later entry and should concentrate on customer services and product design tailored to customer needs.

In making decisions on elements of the marketing mix, it appears that attention to the level of relative price and relative quality might improve financial performance without necessarily harming relative share performance. In general, the relative share rewards from substantially lower relative prices were not significant. Such entrants could have raised their prices somewhat and used the extra margin for customer and technical development or for more rapid expansion. Similarly, the rewards from substantially higher relative quality were not significantly better than those from moderately higher quality. Several entrants appear to have overlooked that many customers make a combined judgment on price and quality; that is, they evaluate the two elements as a single package. Judging by this sample, it appears that the preferred package is moderately better quality at a price close to the existing price level. Substantially higher price and quality combinations were somewhat less rewarding.

The management implications from the data on incumbent reaction are related to the type of relatedness and mode of entry and the amount of probable share loss by the incumbents. Forward integration and technology entrants, who also represent most of the incrementally innovative entrants, should plan on seeing reaction within the first two years. Likewise, entrants who expect that their entry will take away 10 percent share or more from incumbents will also experience reaction within the first two years. These implications amount to the not surprising conclusion that if an entrant sets new standards in a product-market or takes share away from incumbents, some reaction is likely.

At the same time, as noted in chapter 10, the absolute amount of reaction appeared to be small and did not substantially influence performance. There is danger in these data if they were interpreted by managers of future entrants to indicate that reaction need not be allowed for in preentry planning. It must be recalled that the average entry production scale of this sample of entrants was not substantial. It seems likely that if the earlier suggestion to increase scale, and therefore take away more share from incumbents, is followed, then reaction could be larger absolutely and present more of a problem.

IMPLICATIONS FOR INDUSTRIAL ORGANIZATION ECONOMICS

To the extent that this sample is representative of entry by established firms, it appears that managers do not choose to enter mature markets.[2] Only six entrants, or 15 percent of the sample, entered markets in this stage of development. The mature market is the closest to the market situation that is the setting for equilibrium analysis. One implication from this research is, therefore, that much of the theoretical work on entry and reaction is devoted to the case that appears least important in business practice. This implication suggests that economists' preference for static situations should be replaced by dynamic situations. Such a substitution would lead to a better theoretical understanding of the disaggregated economy and the eventual derivation of normative guidelines of value to practitioners.

An additional implication in the same spirit is that theorizing on reaction has been overly narrow in its concentration on price and output. Incumbents can react on exactly the same strategic, or conduct, variables that are available to entrants. To assert, therefore, on the basis of little or no price reaction, that reaction has not occurred is a gross mistruth. Indeed, in this sample, more entrants experienced reaction on product, capacity, and marketing expenditures than on price.

It is recognized that both these implications raise serious methodological problems. Moving from static to dynamic situations and from two variable to multivariate analysis raises problems for traditional microeconomic analysis. Nevertheless, the move is being made in other branches

---

2. Again, a sample of acquisitions might indicate that established firms did enter mature markets (but see the definition of entry in chapter 1).

and it appears just as necessary in the study of the disaggregated behavior of a mixed economy.

IMPLICATIONS FOR PUBLIC POLICY

Lack of entrants into mature markets raises an important public policy issue. The role assigned to entry in economic theory—to help attainment of competitive markets—was not a contingency construct: entry is supposed to occur whenever and wherever profits are above some concept of "normal"[3] (for example, the economywide average or the rate of interest plus a few points for risk). The descriptive finding in this study is that entry occurs primarily into growth markets. It is possible that managers avoid mature markets, even those with a rate of return well above "normal," because as Marris (1964) puts it, "the conflict situation is necessarily intense" (p. 194). Although this sample of results did not show significantly inferior performance from entry into mature markets (but the sample size was only six), it seems reasonable to judge that managers perceive higher risks in entering mature markets.

If managers do, in general, avoid entry into mature markets, then above-normal rates of return could persist in such markets for many years. This practice might explain the lack of entry into industries frequently under congressional and agency scrutiny for "lack of competitiveness": for example, autos and cereals.[4] Rather than investigating alleged collusive or "unconscious shared monopolistic" practices by incumbents alone, such scrutiny should be broadened to include the point of view of potential entrants: what they might gain from entry into a mature market with an above normal rate of return is a question that

---

3. Care has to be used in the application of this concept. For example, the drug industry is often cited as earning above-normal profits. If, however, expenditures on R&D are capitalized, then average drug company rate of return drops from approximately 21 percent to 14 percent and the average for all U.S. manufacturing drops from 11 percent to 9 percent (see Friedman 1973). What is "normal" is not standard across all industries and all types of risk.

4. Although both these cases raise the question, "entry from whom?" the auto industry has experienced entry from foreign producers and the cereal industry has experienced entry from substitute products (such as instant breakfast).

also needs answering. In other words, managers do not calculate just the size of the opportunity but also the probability of attaining it. The combination of size and probability produces, of course, the expected value of the opportunity. This latter calculation, appropriately discounted, is a larger influence on managers than some absolute industry rate of return.

One explanation of a low expected value of entry is that incumbents have erected high barriers to entry, either in collusion or through oligopolistic unconscious parallelism. An alternative reason is that the product and market technology is mature, by definition. Consequently, there is little new that an entrant can offer. In this connection, it is worth recalling that about two-thirds of this sample entered with an incremental innovation while only one-third imitated. Of the fourteen imitators, twelve entered in the growth stage of the life cycle, thus being able to benefit from an increase in primary demand. These numbers mean that only two entrants out of forty chose to imitate in a mature market and rely on obtaining selective demand.

The point of these considerations is that if current product and market technology has been exploited, there is little justification for a new entrant. From the point of view of the business practitioner, an imitative entry into a mature market situation is likely to have a low expected value. From the point of view of public policy, imitative entry into a mature market is likely to increase those activities about which there is considerable agency concern: for example, brand proliferation and escalating marketing expenditures as rivals engage in a selective demand contest.

If there are, therefore, rational reasons for the lack of entry into mature markets, as I believe there are, the public policy issue of above-normal rate of returns still remains. Can incumbents in mature markets price above marginal cost with impunity? In the short run the answer may be yes, within reason. In the long run, the answer is no because current product and market technology will give way to new technology eventually. New technology does two things: it provides a basis for an entrant to offer something different which, in turn, raises the expected value of entry; and second, it creates a new source of potential entrants, that is, those firms that can exploit the new technology. For example, the development of semi-conductors has transformed the calculator product-market from a mature situation to one of the most rapidly growing product-markets in the economy today. The entrants are semiconductor companies, and they, not the mechanical office machine companies, now dominate the field. An example of market technology enabling transformation and a new source of entrant is the Timex entry into watches by taking advantage of the development of mass distribution outlets (who, incidentally, now face, in turn, entry from semiconductor companies with digital watch product technology).

The question of how long is "long" still has to be answered, along with the related question of how long society will tolerate "above-normal" returns while waiting for technology to produce entrants. If society concludes that technology is not acting quickly enough to produce entrants into some industries, then I would rather see action taken to encourage technology and managerial risk taking instead of the current emphasis on the regulation of the strategies of incumbents. This suggestion is not a plea for yet more activist government. It is quite probable that a reduction in current cost-increasing government activities and corporate income tax (but retaining taxation of dividends) would free up corporate funds for R&D and encourage corporate entrepreneurship.

Another public policy implication is that cross-business subsidization (meaning here the same as cross-product subsidization) by established firms has favorable aspects as well as the more commonly expressed unfavorable aspects. Clearly, few of these entrant businesses would have been able to rely on funding from the capital market. A likely rebuttal of this claimed benefit for cross-business subsidization is that entrant difficulties are a sign of product and capital market deficiencies. The product-market that was entered, this argument would hold, contained insuperable barriers to entry and strong, probably collusive, reaction from incumbents. But the previous chapters indicated that difficulties arose not so much from incumbents' "ganging up" on the entrant, the usual naive conception of the entrant's problem in theory. Rather, entrants' difficulties are inherent in starting up something new: these difficulties are the initial, inevitable stages of a new learning curve—the process of "debugging" an incremental innovation. Consequently, poor judgments and decisions occur, such as entering too small, misjudging the impact of rapid market growth, and miscalculating relative price and quality levels. There is, therefore, a "natural" as opposed to a "malevolent" explanation for entrants' difficulties in product-markets. Furthermore, the continuation of these difficulties is likely unless more research of the kind reported here can be accomplished.

The capital market cannot be excused so directly. The established firm, through cross-business subsidization, does provide an environment in which these inevitable initial stages of a new learning curve can be worked out— early mistakes can be tolerated; some extra time to "make good" provided. Capital markets do not provide this environment. If the lack of this environment is a deficiency, then, it follows, the economy needs another deficiency, cross-business subsidization, to provide entrants into many industries. It appears appropriate to conclude as we began: "If the big business is important as a centre of economic power, it is also one of the sources of competition" (chapter 1 above; P. W. S. Andrews 1959). This conclusion does not, of course, necessarily imply acceptance of the current sizes of big business; it simply says that some size beyond that imagined in the perfect competition model may be required.

FUTURE RESEARCH

As in any exploratory research, this study appears to have raised more questions than it answered. The more important research topics will be briefly discussed here.

This research has had to work with a small sample size. The basic question—What kind of entry strategy, in what kind of market, for what kind of parent company skills, against what kind of competitors is likely to succeed?— remains to be answered. A much larger sample size (eighty or more) is required to investigate this question adequately. Unfortunately, the importance of the question is not matched by the practicality of obtaining a larger sample size.

Another area of needed research concerns the influence of organization structure, reporting relationships, and evaluation criteria on the performance of entrant businesses. The chosen entry strategy must, of course, be implemented: resources must be assigned, jobs must be identified and filled, and a means of tracking progress devised. At the same time, an entrant business must satisfy an internal constituency—the executive officers of the parent company. It is probable that attempts to satisfy the internal constituency influence the efforts of an entrant business to satisfy its external constituency.

The public policy implications call for research into the role of technology in providing entrants and into how technology advances may be more economically transferred to the marketplace. Business has been a remarkable agent in the commercialization of research. If, however, the corporate climate for innovation becomes less receptive, as it might in the face of rising risks, interest rates, and these results, then both the growth and the competitiveness of the economy may suffer.

It is hoped that the research reported here will serve as a basis for further study of entry by established firms.

Bibliography

Abell, Derek. "Competitive Market Strategies." Working paper, Marketing Science Institute, Cambridge, Mass., April 1975.

Alemson, M. "Advertising and the Nature of Competition in Oligopoly Over Time: A Case Study." *Economic Journal* (June 1970): 282–306.

———. "Demand, Entry and the Game of Conflict in Oligopoly Over Time: Recent Australian Experience." *Oxford Economic Papers* (July 1969): 220–243.

Andrews, P. W. S. *Manufacturing Business* (London: Macmillan, 1959).

———. *On Competition in Economic Theory* (London: Macmillan, 1964).

———. "Industrial Analysis in Economics." In *Oxford Studies in the Price Mechanism*, ed. T. Wilson and P. W. S. Andrews (Oxford: Clarendon Press, 1951).

Andrews, K. *The Concept of Corporate Strategy* (Homewood: Dow-Jones Irwin, 1971).

Ansoff, Igor H. *Corporate Strategy* (New York: McGraw Hill, 1965).

———. "Strategies for Diversification." *Harvard Business Review* (September-October 1957): 113–124.

Bain, J. *Barriers to New Competition* (Cambridge, Mass.: Harvard University Press, 1956).

———. *Industrial Organization* (New York: Wiley, 1968).

Bevan, Alan. "The UK Potato Crisp Industry, 1960–72: A Study of New Entry Competition." *Journal of Industrial Economics* (June 1974): 281–297.

Bhagwati, Jagdish N. "Oligopoly Theory, Entry-Prevention, and Growth." *Oxford Economic Papers* (November 1970): 297–310.

Bloch, H. "Advertising and Profitability: A Reappraisal." *Journal of Political Economy* (May 1974): 267–268.

Borden, Neil H. "The Concept of the Marketing Mix." *Journal of Advertising Research* (June 1964): 2–7.

Boston Consulting Group. *Perspectives on Experience* (Boston: BCG, 1970).

Bower, Joseph L. *Managing the Resource Allocation Process* (Homewood: Richard D. Irwin, 1972).

Brock, Gerald W. *The U.S. Computer Industry: A Study of Market Power* (Cambridge: Ballinger, 1975).

Brunner, E. "A Note on Potential Competition." *Journal of Industrial Economics* (March 1961): 248–250.

Business Week. "The Rebuilding Job at National Cash Register." May 26, 1973a: 82–86.

Business Week. "The Rebuilding Job at General Foods." August 25, 1973b: 48–55.

Business Week. "ITT: The View from Inside." November 3, 1973c: 42–63.

Business Week. "Innovation." October 12, 1974: 28–29.

Business Week. "A Price War Staggers Bowmar." February 24, 1975: 28.

Buzzell, Robert D., and Nourse, Robert E. M. *Product Innovation in Food Processing, 1954–1964* (Boston: Harvard Business School, Division of Research, 1967).

Buzzell, Robert D.; Gale, Bradley T.; and Sultan, Ralph G. M. "Market Share: A Key to Profitability." *Harvard Business Review* (January–February 1975): 97–106.

Buzzell, Robert D.; Nourse, Robert E. M.; Mathews, John B., Jr.; and Levitt, Theodore. *Marketing: A Contemporary Analysis* (New York: McGraw-Hill, 1972).

Carter, Anne P. "The Economics of Technological Change." *Scientific American* (April 1966): 25–31.

Caves, R. E., and Porter, M. E. "From Entry Barriers to Mobility Barriers: Conjectural Decisions and Contrived Deterrance to New Competition." Discussion Paper no. 40, Harvard Institute of Economic Research, Cambridge, Mass., January 1975.

Caves, R. E. *American Industry: Structure, Conduct, Performance*, 3rd ed. (Englewood Cliffs: Prentice-Hall, 1972).

Chamberlin, E. H. *Theory of Monopolistic Competition*, 8th ed. (Cambridge, Mass.: Harvard University Press, 1962).

Chandler, Alfred D. *Strategy and Structure* (Cambridge, Mass.: MIT Press, 1962).

Copeland, M. "Relation of Consumers' Buying Habits to Marketing Methods." *Harvard Business Review* (April 1923): 282–289.

Cox, William E., Jr. "Product Portfolio Strategy: An Analysis of the Boston Consulting Group Approach to Marketing Strategies." Proceedings of the American Marketing Association, 1974.

Cyert, R. M., and March, J. G., *A Behavioral Theory of the Firm* (Englewood Cliffs: Prentice-Hall, 1963).

Dean, Joel. *Managerial Economics* (Englewood Cliffs: Prentice-Hall, 1951).

———. "Pricing Policies for New Products." *Harvard Business Review* (November-December 1950): 228.

Edwards, Corwin D. "Conglomerate Bigness as a Source of Power." In *Business Concentration and Price Policy*, ed. G. J. Stigler (Princeton: Princeton University Press, 1955).

Ehrenberg, A. S. C. *Data Reduction* (London: Wiley, 1975).

Electronic News. "Minicalculators." January 10, 1972.

Fellner, William. *Competition Among the Few* (New York: Knopf, 1949).

Foote, Nelson. "Market Segmentation as a Competitive Strategy." In *Market Segmentation: Concepts and Applications*, ed. Engel, Fiorillo, and Cayleg (New York: Holt Rinehart & Winston, 1972).

Fortune Magazine. "The Two Faces of Xerox." September 1974: 116–125, 190–198.

Fortune Magazine. "The Nervous Chemical Boom in Chemicals." February 1976: 96–159.

Friedman, Jesse J., and Associates. "R&D Intensity in the Pharmaceutical Industry." Report, Washington, D.C., September 1, 1973.

Fruhan, William. "Pyrrhic Victories in Fights for Market Share." Harvard Business Review (September-October 1972): 100–107.

Gorecki, Paul K. "The determinants of entry by new and diversifying enterprises in the UK manufacturing sector, 1958–1963." *Journal of Applied Economics* (July 1975): 139–147.

Gort, Michael. *Diversification and Integration in American Industry* (Princeton: Princeton University Press, 1962).

Graham, M. "Oligopolistic Reaction and Entry into the USA." Doctoral thesis, Harvard Business School, Boston, 1974.

Hefelbower, Richard B. "Toward a Theory of Industrial Markets and Prices." *American Economic Review—Proceedings* (May 1954): 121–160.

Hines, Howard. "Effectiveness of Entry by Already Established Firms." *Quarterly Journal of Economics* (February 1957): 132–150.

Holton, R. H. "The Distinctions between Convenience Goods, Shopping Goods, and Specialty Goods." *Journal of Marketing* (July 1958): 53–56.

Kamerschen, D. R. "Market Growth and Industry Concentration." *Journal of the American Statistical Association* (March 1968): 228–241.

Kaysen, Carl, and Turner, Donald F. *Antitrust Policy* (Cambridge, Mass.: Harvard University Press, 1959).

Knickerbocker, F. T. *Oligopolistic Reaction and Multinational Enterprise,* (Boston: Harvard Business School, Division of Research, 1973).

Kline, Charles H. "The Strategy of Product Policy." *Harvard Business Review* (July-August 1955): 92–102.

Kotler, Phillip. *Marketing Management* (Englewood Cliffs: Prentice-Hall, 1972).

Kotrba, R. William. "The Strategy Selection Chart." *Journal of Marketing* (July 1966): 22–25.

Kottke, F. J. "Market Entry and the Character of Competition." *Western Economic Journal* (December 1966): 24–43.

Lanzillotti, Robert F. "Multiple Products and Oligopoly Strategy: A Development of Chamberlin's Theory of Products." *Quarterly Journal of Economics* (August 1954): 461–474.

Levitt, Theodore. *Innovation in Marketing* (New York: McGraw-Hill, 1962).

Markham, J. *Conglomerate Enterprise & Public Policy* (Boston: Harvard Business School, Division of Research, 1973).

―――. "The Nature and Significance of Price Leadership." *American Economic Review* (December 1951): 891–905.

Marris, Robin. *The Economic Theory of Managerial Capitalism* (New York: Basic Books, 1968).

Mickwitz, Gosta. *Marketing and Competition* (English Translation). (Ann Arbor: University Microfilms, 1959).

Marketing Science Institute. "Product Life Cycles." Special Report, Cambridge, Mass., 1969.

Menge, J. A. "Style Change Costs as a Market Weapon." *Quarterly Journal of Economics* (November 1962): 632–647.

McGuckin, Robert. "Entry, Concentration Change, and Stability of Market Shares." *Southern Economic Journal* (January 1972): 363–370.

Modigliani, Franco. "New Developments on the Oligopoly Front." *Journal of Political Economy* (June 1958): 215–232.

Needham, Douglas. *Economic Analysis and Industrial Structure,* (New York: Holt, Rinehart and Winston, 1969).

Orr, Dale. "The Determinants of Entry: A Study of the Canadian Manufacturing Industries." *Review of Economics and Statistics* (February 1974): 48–66.

Penrose, Edith T. *The Theory of Growth of the Firm.* (London: Blackwell, 1959).

Porter, Michael E. *Interbrand Choice, Strategy and Bilateral Market Power* (Cambridge, Mass.: Harvard University Press, 1977).

Rumelt, Richard. *Strategy, Structure & Performance* (Boston: Harvard Business School, Division of Research, 1974).

Scherer, F. M. *Industrial Market Structure and Market Performance* (Chicago: Rand McNally, 1971).

Scheuble, Philip A. "ROI for New-Product Planning." *Harvard Business Review* (November–December 1964): 110–120.

Schoeffler, S.; Buzzell, Robert D.; and Heany, Donald F. "Impact of Strategic Planning on Profit Performance." *Harvard Business Review* (March–April 1974): 137–145.

Scott, Bruce R. "Stages of Corporate Development." Unpublished Paper, Harvard Business School, Boston, 1970.

Siegfried, John J., and Weiss, Leonard W. "Advertising, Profits and Corporate Taxes Revisited." *Review of Economics and Statistics* (May 1974): 195–200.

Smith, Wendell R. "Product Differentiation and Market Segmentation as Alternative Market Strategies." *Journal of Marketing* (July 1956): 3–8.

Smith, David K. "The Problems of a New Firm in an Oligopolistic Industry." Doctoral thesis, Harvard Graduate School of Arts and Sciences, Cambridge, Mass., 1951.

Spence, Michael. "Entry, Capacity, Investment and Oligopolistic Pricing." Technical Report no. 131, Institute for Mathematical Studies in the Social Sciences, Stanford University, Palo Alto, Calif., April 1974.

Stigler, G. J. *The Theory of Price* (New York: MacMillan, 1952).

———. *The Theory of Price*, 3rd ed. (New York: MacMillan, 1966).

Sylos-Labini, P. *Oligopoly and Technical Progress* (Milan: Guiffre, 1956), English Translation by Elizabeth Henderson. (Cambridge, Mass.: Harvard University Press, 1962).

Trevelyan, E. W. "The Strategic Process in Large Complex Organizations: A Pilot Study of New Business Development." Doctoral thesis, Harvard Business School, Boston, 1974.

Vernon, Raymond. "Strategies of the Firm." Draft paper. Harvard Business School, Boston, 1974.

Wenders, John T. "Collusion and Entry." *Journal of Political Economy* (November 1971): 1258–77.

Weiss, Leonard W. "Quantitative Studies of Industrial Organization." In *Frontiers of Quantitative Economics* ed. M. D. Intriligator (Amsterdam: North Holland Publishing, 1971).

———. "Advertising, Profits and Corporate Taxes." *Review of Economics and Statistics* (November 1969): 421–430.

Wrigley, Leonard. "Divisional Autonomy and Diversification." Doctoral thesis, Harvard Business School, Boston, 1970.

Zaltman, Gerald, and Burger, Philip C. *Marketing Research* (Hinsdale: Dryden Press, 1975).

Index